Compact Guide to

Colorado
BIRDS

Michael Roedel, Krista Kagume
& Gregory Kennedy

LONE
PINE

Lone Pine Publishing International

© 2007 by Lone Pine Publishing International Inc.
First printed in 2007 10 9 8 7 6 5 4 3
Printed in China

The Distributor: Lone Pine Publishing
1808 B Street NW, Suite 140
Auburn, WA, USA 98001

Website: www.lonepinepublishing.com

Library and Archives Canada Cataloguing in Publication

Roedel, Michael, 1955–
      Compact guide to Colorado birds / Michael Roedel, Krista Kagume, Gregory Kennedy.

Includes index.
ISBN-13: 978-976-8200-22-8

      1. Birds—Colorado—Identification. 2. Bird watching—Colorado.
I. Kennedy, Gregory, 1956– II. Kagume, Krista III. Title.

QL684.C6R63 2007   598.09788   C2006-905110-0

Illustrations: Gary Ross, Ted Nordhagen, Ewa Pluciennik
Egg Photography: Alan Bibby, Gary Whyte
Cover Illustration: Great Horned Owl by Gary Ross
Scanning & Digital Film: Elite Lithographers Co.

We wish to thank the Royal Alberta Museum for providing access to their egg collections.

PC: P13

Contents

WATERFOWL

Snow Goose
size 32 in • p. 20

Canada Goose
size 42 in • p. 22

Mallard
size 24 in • p. 24

Northern Pintail
size 28 in • p. 26

Common Goldeneye
size 18 in • p. 28

Common Merganser
size 25 in • p. 30

GROUSE & QUAIL

Ring-necked Pheasant
size 34 in • p. 32

White-tailed Ptarmigan
size 12 in • p. 34

Dusky Grouse
size 20 in • p. 36

Wild Turkey
size 39 in • p. 38

Scaled Quail
size 11 in • p. 40

Eared Grebe
size 13 in • p. 42

DIVING BIRDS

Western Grebe
size 25 in • p. 44

American White Pelican
size 63 in • p. 46

Double-crested Cormorant
size 29 in • p. 48

HERONS, IBISES & VULTURES

Great Blue Heron
size 51 in • p. 50

Cattle Egret
size 20 in • p. 52

Black-crowned Night-Heron
size 24 in • p. 54

White-faced Ibis
size 23 in • p. 56

Turkey Vulture
size 28 in • p. 58

Bald Eagle
size 36 in • p. 60

Red-tailed Hawk
size 21 in • p. 62

Ferruginous Hawk
size 23 in • p. 64

American Kestrel
size 8 in • p. 66

Prairie Falcon
size 15 in • p. 68

American Coot
size 15 in • p. 70

Sandhill Crane
size 45 in • p. 72

Killdeer
size 10 in • p. 74

American Avocet
size 18 in • p. 76

Spotted Sandpiper
size 8 in • p. 78

Lesser Yellowlegs
size 11 in • p. 80

Wilson's Phalarope
size 9 in • p. 82

Franklin's Gull
size 14 in • p. 84

Ring-billed Gull
size 19 in • p. 86

Black Tern
size 10 in • p. 88

Forster's Tern
size 15 in • p. 90

PIGEONS & DOVES

Rock Pigeon
size 13 in • p. 92

Band-tailed Pigeon
size 14 in • p. 94

Mourning Dove
size 12 in • p. 96

OWLS

Western Screech-Owl
size 9 in • p. 98

Eastern Screech-Owl
size 9 in • p. 100

Great Horned Owl
size 22 in • p. 102

NIGHTJARS & HUMMINGBIRDS

Burrowing Owl
size 10 in • p. 104

Northern Saw-whet Owl
size 8 in • p. 106

Common Nighthawk
size 9 in • p. 108

White-throated Swift
size 7 in • p. 110

Black-chinned Hummingbird
size 3 in • p. 112

Broad-tailed Hummingbird
size 4 in • p. 114

WOODPECKERS

Rufous Hummingbird
size 3 in • p. 116

Red-headed Woodpecker
size 9 in • p. 118

Red-naped Sapsucker
size 8 in • p. 120

FLYCATCHERS

Downy Woodpecker
size 7 in • p. 122

Northern Flicker
size 13 in • p. 124

Western Wood-Pewee
size 6 in • p. 126

Dusky Flycatcher
size 6 in • p. 128

Say's Phoebe
size 7 in • p. 130

Western Kingbird
size 9 in • p. 132

FLYCATCHERS

Loggerhead Shrike
size 9 in • p. 134

Warbling Vireo
size 5 in • p. 136

Steller's Jay
size 12 in • p. 138

STRIKES & VIREOS

Pinyon Jay
size 11 in • p. 140

Clark's Nutcracker
size 13 in • p. 142

Black-billed Magpie
size 18 in • p. 144

JAYS & RAVENS

Common Raven
size 22 in • p. 146

Horned Lark
size 7 in • p. 148

Purple Martin
size 8 in • p. 150

LARKS & SWALLOWS

Cliff Swallow
size 5 in • p. 152

Barn Swallow
size 7 in • p. 154

Mountain Chickadee
size 5 in • p. 156

CHICKADEES, NUTHATCHES & WRENS

White-breasted Nuthatch
size 5 in • p. 158

Rock Wren
size 6 in • p. 160

House Wren
size 5 in • p. 162

American Dipper
size 7 in • p. 164

Ruby-crowned Kinglet
size 4 in • p. 166

Mountain Bluebird
size 7 in • p. 168

Hermit Thrush
size 7 in • p. 170

American Robin
size 10 in • p. 172

Northern Mockingbird
size 10 in • p. 174

Sage Thrasher
size 8 in • p. 176

European Starling
size 8 in • p. 178

Cedar Waxwing
size 7 in • p. 180

Yellow Warbler
size 5 in • p. 182

Yellow-rumped Warbler
size 5 in • p. 184

Wilson's Warbler
size 5 in • p. 186

Yellow-breasted Chat
size 7 in • p. 188

Western Tanager
size 7 in • p. 190

Green-tailed Towhee
size 7 in • p. 192

Spotted Towhee
size 8 in • p. 194

Chipping Sparrow
size 6 in • p. 196

Lark Bunting
size 7 in • p. 198

Song Sparrow
size 6 in • p. 200

White-crowned Sparrow
size 6 in • p. 202

Dark-eyed Junco
size 7 in • p. 204

Black-headed Grosbeak
size 8 in • p. 206

Blue Grosbeak
size 7 in • p. 208

Lazuli Bunting
size 5 in • p. 210

Red-winged Blackbird
size 8 in • p. 212

Western Meadowlark
size 9 in • p. 214

Yellow-headed Blackbird
size 10 in • p. 216

Brown-headed Cowbird
size 8 in • p. 218

Bullock's Oriole
size 9 in • p. 220

Gray-crowned Rosy-Finch
size 6 in • p. 222

Pine Siskin
size 5 in • p. 224

American Goldfinch
size 5 in • p. 226

House Sparrow
size 6 in • p. 228

Introduction

If you have ever admired a songbird's pleasant notes, been fascinated by a soaring hawk or wondered the identity of the birds at your backyard feeder, this book is for you. There is so much to discover about birds and their surroundings that birding is becoming one of the fastest growing hobbies on the planet. Many people find it relaxing, while others enjoy its outdoor appeal. Some people see it as a way to reconnect with like-minded people or a way to monitor the environment.

Whether you are just beginning to take an interest in birds or can already identify many species, there is always more to learn. We've highlighted both the remarkable traits and the more typical behaviors displayed by some of our most abundant or noteworthy birds. A few live in specialized habitats, but most are common species that you have a good chance of encountering on most outings or in your backyard.

Downy Woodpecker

BIRDING IN COLORADO

We are truly blessed by the geographical and biological diversity of Colorado. In addition to supporting a wide range of breeding birds and year-round residents, our state hosts a large number of spring and fall migrants that move through our region on the way to their breeding and wintering grounds. In all, over 470 bird species have been seen and recorded in Colorado.

Identifying birds in action and under varying conditions involves skill, timing and luck. The more you know about a bird, its range, preferred habitat, food preferences and hours and seasons of activity, the better your chances will be of seeing it. Generally, spring and fall are the busiest birding times. Temperatures are moderate then, many species of birds are on the move, and in spring, male songbirds are belting out their unique courtship songs. Birds are usually most active in the early morning hours, except in winter when they forage during the day when milder temperatures prevail.

Another useful clue for correctly recognizing birds is knowledge of their habitat. Simply put, a bird's habitat is the place where it normally lives. Some birds prefer open water, some are found in cattail marshes, others like mature coniferous forest, and still other birds prefer abandoned agricultural fields overgrown with tall grass and shrubs. Habitats are just like neighborhoods: if you associate friends with the suburb in which they live, you can easily learn to associate specific birds with their preferred habitat. Only in migration, especially during inclement weather, do some birds leave their usual habitat.

Recognizing birds by their songs and calls can greatly enhance your birding experience. Numerous tapes and CDs are available to help you learn bird songs, and a portable player with headphones can let you quickly compare a live bird with a recording. The old-fashioned way to remember bird songs is to make up phrases for them. We have given you some of the classic renderings in

Cedar Waxwing

the species accounts that follow. Some of these approximations work better than others; birds often add or delete syllables from their calls, and very few pronounce consonants in a recognizable fashion. Remember, too, that songs may vary from place to place.

Colorado has a long tradition of friendly, recreational birding. In general, birders are willing to help beginners, share their knowledge and involve novices in their projects. Christmas bird counts, breeding bird surveys, nest box programs, migration monitoring and birding lectures and workshops provide a chance for birders of all levels to interact and share the splendor of birds. Bird hotlines provide up-to-date information on the sightings of rarities, which are often easier to relocate than you might think. For more information or to participate in these projects, contact the following organizations:

Colorado Field Ornithologists (CFO)
P.O. Box 481
Lyons, CO   80540
Website: http://www.cfo-link.org

Colorado Birding Society
1269 South Blackhawk Way
Aurora, CO   80012-4657
Website: http://home.att.net/~birdertoo

Rocky Mountain Bird Observatory
14500 Lark Bunting Lane
Brighton, CO   80603-8311
Phone: (303) 659-4348
Website: http://www.rmbo.org

Audubon Colorado
1966, 13th Street, Suite 230
Boulder, CO   80302-5217
Phone: (303) 415-0130
Website: http://co.audubon.org

Colorado Division of Wildlife
Website: http://wildlife.state.co.us

BIRD LISTING

Many birders list the species they have seen during excursions or at home. It is up to you to decide what kind of list—systematic or casual—you will keep, and you may choose not to make lists at all. Lists may prove rewarding in unexpected ways, and after you visit a new area, your list becomes a souvenir of your experiences there. Keeping regular, accurate lists of birds in your neighborhood can also be useful for local researchers. It can be interesting to compare the arrival dates and last sightings of hummingbirds and other seasonal visitors, or to note the first sighting of a new visitor to your area.

BIRD FEEDING

Many people set up bird feeders in their backyard, especially in winter. It is possible to attract specific birds by choosing the right kind of food and style of feeder. Keep your feeder stocked through late spring, because birds have a hard time finding food before the flowers bloom, seeds develop and insects hatch. Contrary to popular opinion, birds do not become dependent on feeders, nor

Western Meadowlark

do they subsequently forget to forage naturally. Clean your feeder and the surrounding area regularly to prevent the spread of disease.

Landscaping your property with native plants is another way of providing natural food for birds. Flocks of waxwings have a keen eye for red mountain-ash berries and hummingbirds enjoy columbine flowers. The cumulative effects of "nature-scaping" urban yards can be a significant step toward habitat conservation (especially when you consider that habitat is often lost in small amounts—a power line is cut in one area and a highway is built in another). Many good books and websites about attracting wildlife to your backyard are available.

NEST BOXES

Another popular way to attract birds is to put up nest boxes, especially for bluebirds and Purple Martins. Not all birds will use nest boxes: only species that normally use cavities in trees are comfortable in such confined spaces. Larger nest boxes can attract kestrels, owls and cavity-nesting ducks.

CLEANING NEST BOXES AND FEEDERS

Nest boxes and feeding stations must be kept clean to prevent birds from becoming ill or spreading disease. Old nesting material may harbor a number of parasites. Once the birds have left for the season, remove the nesting material and wash and scrub the nest box with detergent or a 10 percent bleach solution (1 part bleach to 9 parts water). You can also scald the nest box with boiling water. Rinse it well and let it dry thoroughly before you remount it.

Unclean bird feeders can become contaminated with salmonellosis and possibly other diseases. Seed feeders should be cleaned monthly; hummingbird feeders at least weekly. Any seed, fruit or suet that is moldy or spoiled must be discarded. Clean and disinfect feeding stations with a 10 percent bleach solution, scrubbing thoroughly. Rinse the feeder well and allow it to dry completely before refilling it. Discarded seed and feces on the ground under the feeding station should also be removed.

We advise that you wear rubber gloves and a mask when cleaning nest boxes or feeders.

WEST NILE VIRUS

Since the West Nile Virus first surfaced in North America in 1999, it has caused fear and misunderstanding. Some people have become afraid of contracting the disease from birds, and some health departments have advised residents to eliminate feeding stations and birdbaths.

To date, the disease has reportedly killed over 280 species of birds. Corvids (crows, jays and ravens) and birds of prey have been the most obvious victims because of their size, though the disease also affects some smaller species. The virus is transmitted among birds and to humans (as well as some other mammals) by mosquitoes that have bitten infected birds. Birds do not get the disease directly from other birds, and humans cannot get it from casual contact with infected birds. As well, not all mosquito species can carry the disease. According to the Centers for Disease Control and Prevention (CDC), only about 20 percent of people who are bitten and become infected will develop any symptoms at all and less than 1 percent will become severely ill.

Because mosquitoes breed in standing water, birdbaths have the potential to become mosquito breeding grounds. Birdbaths should be emptied and have the water changed at least weekly. Drippers, circulating pumps, fountains or waterfalls that keep water moving will prevent mosquitoes from laying their eggs in the water. There are also bird-friendly products available to treat water in birdbaths. Contact your local nature store or garden center for more information on these products.

ABOUT THE SPECIES ACCOUNTS

This book gives detailed accounts of 105 species of birds that can be expected in Colorado on an annual basis. The order of the birds and their common and scientific names follow the American Ornithologists' Union's *Check-list of North American Birds* (7th edition, July 1998, and its supplements through 2006).

As well as showing the identifying features of the bird, each species account also attempts to bring the bird to life by describing its various character traits. One of the challenges of birding is that many species look different in spring and summer than they do in fall and winter. Many birds have breeding and nonbreeding plumages, and immature birds often look different from their parents. This book does not try to describe or illustrate all the different plumages of a species; instead, it tries to focus on the forms that are most likely to be seen in our area.

ID: Large illustrations point out prominent field marks that will help you tell each bird apart. The descriptions favor easily understood language instead of technical terms.

Other ID: This section lists additional identifying features. Some of the most common anatomical features of birds are pointed out in the Glossary illustration (p. 231).

Size: The average length of the bird's body from bill to tail, as well as wingspan, are given and are approximate measurements of the bird as it is seen in nature. The size is sometimes given as a range, because there is variation between individuals, or between males and females.

Voice: You will hear many birds, particularly songbirds, that may remain hidden from view. Memorable paraphrases of distinctive sounds will aid you in identifying a species by ear.

Status: A general comment, such as "common," "uncommon" or "rare," is usually sufficient to describe the relative abundance of a species. Situations are bound to vary somewhat, because migratory pulses, seasonal changes and centers of activity tend to concentrate or disperse birds.

Northern Saw-whet Owl

Habitat: This section describes where each species is most commonly found. Because of the freedom that flight gives them, birds can turn up in almost any type of habitat. However, they will usually be found in environments that provide the specific food, water, cover and, in some cases, nesting habitat that they need to survive.

Similar Birds: Easily confused species are illustrated for each account. If you concentrate on the most relevant field marks, the subtle differences between species can be reduced to easily identifiable traits.

Nesting: In each species account, nest location and structure, clutch size, incubation period and parental duties are discussed. A photo of the bird's egg is also provided. Remember that birding ethics discourage the disturbance of active bird nests. If you disturb a nest, you may drive off the parents during a critical period or expose defenseless young to predators.

Range Maps: The range map for each species shows the overall range of the species in an average year. Most birds will confine their annual movements to this range, although each year some birds wander beyond their traditional boundaries. The maps show year-round, summer and winter ranges, as well as migratory pathways (areas of the region where birds may appear while en route to nesting or winter habitat). The representations of the pathways do not distinguish high-use migration corridors from areas that are seldom used.

Range Map Symbols

summer

winter

year-round

migration

TOP BIRDING SITES

From the Rocky Mountains in the west to the plains in the east, our state can be separated into six natural regions: Arizona/New Mexico Plateau, Colorado Plateaus, High Plains, Southern Rockies, Southwestern Tablelands and Wyoming Basin. Each region is composed of a number of different habitats that support a wealth of wildlife.

There are hundreds of good birding areas throughout our region. The following areas have been selected to represent a broad range of bird communities and habitats, with an emphasis on accessibility.

1. Browns Park NWR
2. Steamboat Lake SP
3. Pawnee National Grassland
4. Jumbo Reservoir
5. Jackson Lake SP
6. Bonny Lake SP
7. Rocky Mountain NP
8. Eldorado Canyon SP
9. Bluff Lake Nature Center
10. Cherry Creek SP
11. Colorado National Monument
12. Eleven Mile SP
13. Garden of the Gods
14. Gunnison SWA
15. Fountain Creek Nature Center
16. Kinney Lake SWA
17. Ouray
18. Lake Pueblo SP
19. John Martin Reservoir SP
20. Perins Peak SWA
21. Monte Vista NWR
22. San Luis Lakes
23. Bosque Del Oso SWA
24. Comanche National Grasslands

NP = National Park
NWR = National Wildlife Refuge
SP = State Park
SWA = State Wildlife Area

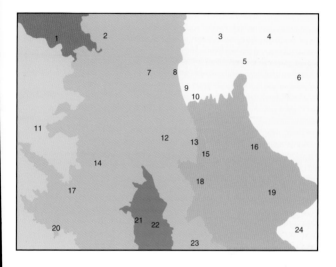

Ecoregions of Colorado

Arizona/New Mexico Plateau
Colorado Plateaus
High Plains
Southern Rockies
Southwestern Tablelands
Wyoming Basin

Snow Goose
Chen caerulescens

Noisy flocks of Snow Geese can be quite entertaining, creating a moving patchwork in the sky with their black wing tips and white plumage. • These geese breed in the Arctic, some traveling as far as northeastern Siberia and crossing the Bering Strait twice a year. Their smiling, serrated bills are made for grazing on short arctic tundra and gripping the slippery roots of marsh plants. • Snow Geese can fly at speeds of up to 20 miles per hour. They are also strong walkers, and mothers have been known to lead their goslings up to 45 miles on foot in search of suitable habitat.

Other ID: head often stained rusty red. *Blue morph:* rare; white head and upper neck; dark blue-gray body.
Size: *L* 30–33 in; W 4½–5 ft.
Voice: loud, nasal, *houk-houk* in flight, higher pitched and more constant than calls of the Canada Goose.
Status: common during winter in the eastern plains.
Habitat: croplands, fields.

Similar Birds

Ross's Goose

American White Pelican
(p. 46)

black wing tips

blue morph

dark "grin" on bill

white morph

Nesting: does not nest in Colorado; nests in the Arctic; female lines a depression with grass, feathers and down; creamy white eggs are 3⅛ x 2 in; female incubates 4–7 eggs for 22–25 days.

Did You Know?

The Snow Goose has two color morphs, a white and a blue, which until 1983 were considered two different species.

Look For

Snow Geese fly in wavy, disorganized lines, whereas Canada Geese fly in a V-formation. Occasionally mixed flocks form in migration.

Canada Goose
Branta canadensis

Canada Geese mate for life and are devoted parents. Unlike most birds, Canada Geese stay together in a family group for nearly a year, which increases the survival rate of the young. • Rescuers who care for injured geese report that these birds readily adopt their human caregivers. However, wild geese can be aggressive, especially when defending young or competing for food. Hissing sounds and low, outstretched necks are signs that you should give these birds some space. • The Canada Goose was split into two species in 2004. The larger subspecies are still known as Canada Geese, whereas the smaller subspecies have been renamed Cackling Geese.

Other ID: dark brown upperparts; light brown underparts; short, black tail. *In flight:* flocks fly in V-formation.
Size: L 3–4 ft; W up to 6 ft.
Voice: loud, familiar *ah-honk.*
Status: abundant year-round resident in appropriate habitat.
Habitat: plains, valleys, lakeshores, riverbanks, ponds, farmlands and city parks.

Similar Birds

Cackling Goose

Greater White-fronted Goose

long, black neck

white
"chin strap"

white undertail
coverts

Nesting: usually on the ground; female builds
a nest of grass and mud, lined with down; white
eggs are 3½ x 2¼ in; female incubates 3–8 eggs
for 25–28 days; goslings are born in May.

Did You Know?

The Canada Goose can
be found in many different
habitats and has the most
widespread distribution of
any North American
goose.

Look For

When on the water, Canada
Geese graze on aquatic
grasses and sprouts. You can
spot them tipping up to grab
for underwater roots and
tubers.

Mallard
Anas platyrhynchos

Mallards can be seen year-round, often in flocks and always near open water. These confident ducks have even been spotted dabbling in out-door swimming pools. • The male Mallard, with his shiny green head and chestnut brown breast, is the classic wild duck. After breeding, the male loses his elaborate plumage, helping him stay cam-ouflaged during a brief flightless period. In early fall, he molts back into breeding colors.

Other ID: orange feet. *Male:* white "necklace"; black tail feathers curl upward. *Female:* mottled brown overall.
Size: *L* 20–28 in; *W* 3 ft.
Voice: quacks; female is louder than male.
Status: abundant year-round resident except at higher elevations.
Habitat: lakes, wetlands, rivers, city parks, agricultural areas and sewage lagoons.

Similar Birds

Northern Shoveler

Common Merganser
(p. 30)

glossy green head

yellow bill

dark blue speculum
bordered by white

orange bill spattered
with black

♂

♀

Nesting: a grass nest is built on the ground or under a bush; creamy, grayish or greenish white eggs are 2¼ x 1⅝ in; female incubates 7–10 eggs for 26–30 days.

Did You Know?

A nesting hen generates enough body heat to make the grass around her nest grow faster. She uses the tall grass to further conceal her precious nest.

Look For

Mallards will readily hybridize with a variety of other duck species, often producing very peculiar plumages.

Northern Pintail
Anas acuta

A long neck and a long, tapered tail put this dabbling duck in a class of its own. The elegant and graceful Northern Pintail is not unique to North America; it also breeds in Asia and northern Europe. • These migrants arrive early to scout out flooded agricultural fields for choice nesting locations. Unfortunately, Northern Pintails usually build their nests in vulnerable areas, on exposed ground near water, which has resulted in a slow decline in their population. Recent efforts to improve habitat though management, as well as harvesting restrictions, are helping to stabilize their numbers.

Other ID: long, slender neck; dark, glossy bill. *Male:* dusty gray body plumage; black and white hindquarters; long, tapering tail feathers. *Female:* mottled, light brown overall.
Size: *Male:* L 25–30 in; W 34 in. *Female:* L 20–22 in; W 34 in.
Voice: *Male:* soft, whistling call.
Female: rough quack.
Status: common migrant statewide; locally common summer resident; rare to uncommon winter resident where open water is available.
Habitat: shallow wetlands, flooded fields and lake edges; also on arctic tundra.

Similar Birds

Northern Shoveler

Gadwall

Blue-winged Teal

chocolate brown head

white on breast extends up sides of neck

Nesting: in a small depression in vegetation; nest of grass, leaves and moss is lined with down; greenish buff eggs are 2⅛ x 1½ in; female incubates 6–12 eggs for 22–25 days.

Did You Know?

The Northern Pintail, one of the most abundant waterfowl species on the continent, migrates at night at altitudes of up to 3000 feet.

Look For

The long, pointed tail of the male Northern Pintail is easily seen in flight and points skyward when the bird tips up to dabble.

Common Goldeneye
Bucephala clangula

The Common Goldeneye typically spends its entire life in North America, dividing its time between breeding grounds in the boreal forests of Canada and Alaska and wintering grounds on reservoirs, lakes, rivers or in marine bays along the Atlantic and Pacific coasts. • Fish, crustaceans and mollusks make up a major portion of the Common Goldeneye's winter diet, but in summer, this diving duck eats a lot of aquatic invertebrates and tubers. • Common Goldeneyes are frequently called "Whistlers," because the wind whistles through their wings when they fly.

Other ID: golden eyes. *Male:* dark, iridescent green head; dark back; white sides and belly. *Female:* lighter breast and belly; gray-brown body plumage; dark bill is tipped with yellow in spring and summer.
Size: L 16–20 in; W 26 in.
Voice: generally silent in migration and winter.
Male: courtship calls are a nasal *peent* and a hoarse *kraaagh. Female:* a harsh croak.
Status: fairly common during winter in appropriate habitat.
Habitat: open water of plains, valleys and parks; lakes, large ponds and rivers.

Similar Birds

Bufflehead

Hooded Merganser

Barrow's Goldeneye

black wings with large, white wing patches ♂

♀

chocolate brown head

steep forehead with peaked crown

white, oval cheek patch

dark bill

♀

♂

Nesting: does not nest in Colorado; nests in Canada and Alaska; in a tree cavity, or occasionally a nest box, lined with wood chips and down; often close to water; blue-green eggs are 2⅜ x 1⅝ in; female incubates 6–10 eggs for 28–32 days.

Did You Know?

In winter, female Common Goldeneyes fly farther south than males, and juvenile birds continue even farther south.

Look For

The largest numbers of Common Goldeneyes are seen in western Colorado during winter, wherever waters remain ice-free.

Common Merganser
Mergus merganser

Lumbering like a jumbo jet, the Common Merganser must run along the surface of the water, beating its heavy wings to gain sufficient lift to take off. Once up and away, this large duck flies arrow-straight and low over the water, making broad, sweeping turns to follow the meandering shorelines of rivers and lakes. • Common Mergansers are highly social and often gather in large groups during migration. In winter, any source of open water with a fish-filled shoal will support good numbers of these skilled divers.

Other ID: large, elongated body. *Male:* white body plumage; black stripe on back; dark eyes. *Female:* gray body; orangy eyes. *In flight:* shallow wingbeats; body is compressed and arrowlike.
Size: L 22–27 in; W 34 in.
Voice: *Male:* harsh *uig-a*, like a guitar twang. *Female:* harsh *karr karr*.
Status: common in migration and winter; less common in summer.
Habitat: large rivers and deep lakes; in plains, valleys and parks during winter.

Similar Birds

Red-breasted Merganser

Northern Shoveler

Common Loon

glossy, green head
without crest

red bill

rusty neck and
crested head

♂

♀

clean white chin
and breast

Nesting: in a tree cavity; occasionally on the ground, on a cliff ledge or in a large nest box; usually close to water; pale buff eggs are 2½ x 1¾ in; female incubates 8–11 eggs for 30–35 days.

Did You Know?

The Common Merganser is the most widespread and abundant merganser in North America. It also occurs in Europe and Asia.

Look For

You may see the Common Merganser with only its head under water, searching for prey. A special serrated bill allows it to grip slippery fish.

Ring-necked Pheasant

Phasianus colchicus

The Ring-necked Pheasant was brought to North America in the late 1800s, mainly as a game bird. Since then, its numbers have had to be continually replenished by hatchery-raised young, not only because it is hunted, but because of diminished habitat, intensive farming practices and harsh winters. • Unlike native grouse, this pheasant does not have feathered legs and feet for insulation, and it cannot live on native plants alone; it depends on grain and corn crops for survival in Colorado.

Other ID: *Male:* bronze underparts. *Female:* mottled brown overall; light underparts.
Size: *Male:* L 30–36 in; W 31 in. *Female:* L 20–26 in; W 28 in.
Voice: *Male:* loud, raspy, roosterlike crowing: *ka-squawk*; whirring of the wings mostly just before sunrise.
Status: fairly common year-round.
Habitat: in plains, valleys, parks, shrubby grasslands, grassy ditches and fencelines, woodlots and croplands.

Similar Birds

Greater Sage-Grouse

Greater Prairie-Chicken

Lesser Prairie-Chicken

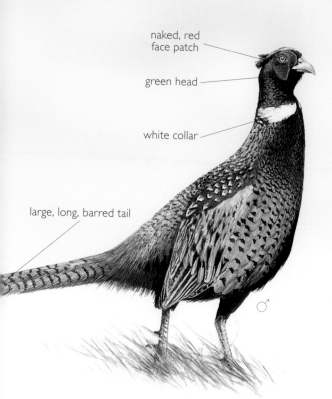

naked, red face patch

green head

white collar

large, long, barred tail

♂

Nesting: on the ground, among vegetation or next to a log or other natural debris; in a slight depression lined with grass and leaves; olive buff eggs are 1¾ x 1⅜ in; female incubates 10–12 eggs for 23–28 days.

Did You Know?

This pheasant does not fly long distances; it exhibits bursts of labored flight that allows it to escape most predators.

Look For

Family groups of young pheasants forage along weedy country roadsides on summer mornings and evenings.

White-tailed Ptarmigan

Lagopus leucura

It would be hard to imagine a better-adapted alpine hiker than the White-tailed Ptarmigan. Its plumage perfectly matches its surroundings, regardless of the season, and in winter its feathered feet look like fluffy bedroom slippers, allowing the ptarmigan to snow-shoe atop the snowdrifts. • Even though a brooding female White-tailed Ptarmigan will remain on her nest if she is closely approached, this is very stressful to her. Sensitive hikers can make a ptarmigan's tough life somewhat easier by keeping a respectful distance.

Other ID: small size. *Breeding male:* white on wings and belly. *Breeding female:* mottled, brown and black overall. *Nonbreeding:* all-white plumage; fully feathered feet.
Size: *L* 12½ in; *W* 22 in.
Voice: *Male:* high-pitched *ku-kriii kriii*; low *kuk-kuk-kuk*. *Female:* low clucks.
Status: common in alpine tundra during summer; locally common near the timberline in winter.
Habitat: alpine areas ranging from dry, rocky areas to mossy streamsides; dwarf willow thickets at or above treeline; might move to lower elevations during winter.

Similar Birds

Dusky Grouse
(p. 36)

Look For

The White-tailed Ptarmigan is the only species of grouse with white tail feathers and is the smallest grouse in North America.

red eyebrow is pronounced during courtship

barred, brown and black "necklace"

♂ black eyes and bill

breeding

white outer tail feathers

Nesting: on the ground, among rocks; in a depression lined with fine grass, leaves and lichens; buff, brown-spotted eggs are 1⅝ x 1¼ in; female incubates 3–9 eggs for 24–26 days.

Did You Know?

In spring, a male will impress a female by flaring his red eyebrows, fanning his tail and dragging his wing tips on the ground. When he thinks he has made an impression, he will walk toward the female. If she runs away, he will often chase after her, emitting a barrage of clucks and chatters.

Dusky Grouse
Dendragapus obscurus

The largest of our mountain grouse, the Dusky Grouse, formerly known as the Blue Grouse, is well adapted to living at the timberline. In winter, additional scales grow around each toe, transforming its specialized feet into "snowshoes."

• Prior to breeding, Dusky Grouse migrate to lower elevations, where the male's deep courting notes signal the arrival of spring. His owl-like hoots are so deep that the human ear can detect only a fraction of the sounds produced.

Other ID: long neck; white undertail coverts; feathered legs. *Male:* blue-gray crown, nape, upper back and tail feathers; when displaying, shows inflated red throat patch surrounded by white feathers. *Female:* blue-gray lower breast and belly; faint yellow comb. *In flight:* tail nearly all dark, or with faint gray subterminal band.

Size: L 17–22 in; W 24–28 in. (male generally larger than female)

Voice: 5–8 extremely deep hoots, the first or second hoot loudest, then trailing off.

Status: fairly common year-round resident at higher elevations.

Habitat: coniferous forests of higher foothills and mountains; often found in burns or other forest clearings.

Similar Birds

White-tailed Ptarmigan
(p. 34)

Look For

This grouse's mottled brown plumage blends in so well with its surroundings that it often freezes when threatened—a habit that has earned it the name "Fool's Hen."

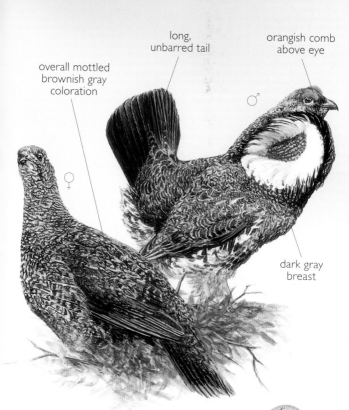

long,
unbarred tail

orangish comb
above eye

overall mottled
brownish gray
coloration

♂

♀

dark gray
breast

Nesting: often near a fallen log or under a shrub; scrape nest is lined with vegetation; brown-speckled, pale pink or buff eggs are 2 x 1½ in; female incubates 7–10 eggs for 25–28 days.

Did You Know?

In winter, the Dusky Grouse dines almost exclusively on conifer needles. To help break down such a fibrous food, it regularly ingests small stones. The grit ingested in fall may remain in the bird's gizzard until spring, at which point the Dusky Grouse varies its diet with leaf buds of deciduous trees, and fruits and berries.

Wild Turkey
Meleagris gallopavo

If Congress had taken Benjamin Franklin's advice in 1782, our national emblem would be the Wild Turkey instead of the Bald Eagle. • This charismatic bird is the only native North American animal that has been widely domesticated. The wild ancestors of most other domestic animals came from Europe. • Wild Turkeys are wary birds with acute senses. They live in groups called "rafters" and have a highly developed social system.

Other ID: dark, glossy, iridescent body plumage; largely unfeathered legs. *Male:* black-tipped breast feathers; colorful head and body. *Female:* smaller; blue-gray head; less iridescent body; brown-tipped breast feathers.
Size: *Male:* L 3–3½ ft; W 5½ ft. *Female:* L 3 ft; W 4 ft.
Voice: courting male gobbles loudly; alarm call is a loud *pert*; gathering call is a cluck; contact call is a loud *keouk-keouk-keouk*.
Status: fairly common year-round resident except at higher elevations.
Habitat: deciduous, mixed and riparian woodlands; occasionally eats waste grain and corn from fields in late fall and winter.

Similar Birds

Ring-necked Pheasant
(p. 32)

Look For

Eastern Wild Turkeys have brown or rusty tail tips and are slimmer than domestic turkeys, which have white tail tips.

naked, blue-red head

barred, copper-colored tail

red wattles

♂

long central breast tassel

Nesting: in a woodland or at a field edge; nests on the ground, in a depression under thick cover; nest is lined with grass and leaves; brown-speckled, pale buff eggs are 2½ x 1¾ in; female incubates 10–12 eggs for up to 28 days.

Did You Know?

The Wild Turkey was once very common throughout most of eastern North America, but during the 20th century, habitat loss and overhunting took a toll on its populations. Today, efforts at restoration have reestablished this species nearly statewide.

Scaled Quail
Callipepla squamata

The Scaled Quail, also called "Cottontop" or "Blue Quail," is a stocky bird with a bushy, white crest. It is found in the arid scrubland habitat of southeastern Colorado. Seeds make up a large part of the Scaled Quail's diet, but insects are also an important source of nutrition and water. • These birds are swift on the ground and prefer to run rather than fly. They require pockets of cover, ranging from short grass to shrubs and brush piles, for escape, roosting, nesting and hiding. Overgrazing and land management for other species often destroys suitable cover.

Other ID: stocky body; pale gray and brown plumage; one white wing bar; gray-tipped tail. *Male:* buffy throat patch; large crest.
Size: L 10–12 in; W 14 in.
Voice: males give a loud *sheesh!*; throaty *chip-Chuk!* when separated; various clicks and trills.
Status: fairly common year-round resident in southeastern Colorado.
Habitat: arid scrub and grasslands; may be found in coveys around log piles or farm equipment; usually within 1–2 mi of water.

Similar Birds

Gambels' Quail, female

Look For

The "scaly" appearance of this bird is the product of black edging along its feathers.

white tuft on head

gray "scales" around neck and down front

♂

white, horizontal stripes along sides

♀

Nesting: on the ground; in a small depression under thick vegetation; white eggs with brown speckling are 1⅜ x 1 in; female incubates 12–14 eggs for 22–23 days as the male defends the nesting territory.

Did You Know?

In winter, Scaled Quails gather into groups, called "coveys," which often include over 30 birds. On cold nights, the birds huddle together in a tight circle with each bird facing outward. This practice enables the group to detect danger from any direction.

Eared Grebe
Podiceps nigricollis

Eared Grebes are common inhabitants of Colorado's larger lakes. The internal organs and pectoral muscles of these birds shrink or swell, depending on whether or not the birds need to migrate. This leaves Eared Grebes flightless for a longer period—nine to ten months annually— than any other flying bird in the world. • Grebes eat feathers, which pack the digestive tract and may protect the stomach lining and intes- tines from sharp fish bones or parasites, or perhaps slow the passage of food, allowing more time for complete digestion.

Other ID: *Nonbreeding:* light underparts; dusky upper fore- neck and flanks. *In flight:* wings beat constantly; hunchbacked appearance; legs trail behind tail.
Size: L 11½–14 in; W 16 in.
Voice: ascending, whistled *ooEET* dur- ing courtship.
Status: fairly common migrant; locally abundant summer resident; locally uncommon to rare in winter.
Habitat: wetlands, large lakes and sewage disposal ponds; in plains, valleys and parks during migration.

Similar Birds

Horned Grebe

Pied-billed Grebe

slightly raised crown

red eyes

fanned-out, golden "ear" tufts

black upperparts

chestnut flanks

thin, straight bill

black neck

breeding

Nesting: usually colonial; on the edge of a lake or wetland; floating platform nest is built among thick vegetation; white eggs are 1⅝ x 1¼ in; pair incubates 3–5 eggs for 20–22 days.

Did You Know?

When the nestlings are 10 days old, the brood is divided and each adult cares for half of the young. At 20 days, the young are left to fend for themselves.

Look For

The scientific name *nigricollis* means "black neck," a characteristic of this bird's breeding plumage.

Western Grebe
Aechmophorus occidentalis

Elegant Western Grebes are famous for their elaborate courtship rituals, in which pairs caress each other with aquatic vegetation and sprint side by side, literally "walking on water." The grebes stand high, feet paddling furiously, with their wings stretched back and heads and necks held rigid, until the race ends with the pair breaking the water's surface in a graceful dive. • Though Western Grebes can be common summer residents in Colorado, many birds are nonbreeders.

Other ID: white underparts from chin to belly; white cheek.
Size: *L* 25 in; *W* 24 in.
Voice: high-pitched, scraping *crreeet-crreeet;* repeated call sounds like a squeaky wheel.
Status: common in migration and summer on eastern plains and western valleys.
Habitat: large, deep lakes and reservoirs.

Similar Birds

Clark's Grebe

Red-necked Grebe

black on face extends below red eyes

long, thin, yellow to dull olive bill

black upperparts from base of bill to tail

long, slender neck

Nesting: usually in colonies; pair builds a floating nest of fresh and decaying vegetation; bluish green to buffy eggs (becoming stained brown) are 2¼ x 1½ in; pair incubates 2–7 eggs for about 23 days.

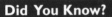

Did You Know?

These birds are fond of a wide variety of fish, which they hunt as they shoot through the water during their underwater dives.

Look For

The Western Grebe looks nearly identical to the Clark's Grebe, but it has a duller bill, a dark patch that extends below the eye and less white on its flight feathers.

American White Pelican
Pelecanus erythrorhynchos

This majestic wetland bird is one of only a few bird species that feeds cooperatively. A group of pelicans will herd fish into a school, then dip their bucketlike bills into the water to capture their prey. In a single scoop of its bill, a pelican can trap over 3 gallons of water and fish, which is about two to three times as much as its stomach can hold. This impressive feat inspired Dixon Lanier Merritt to write: "A wonderful bird is a pelican. His bill will hold more than his belican!"

Other ID: *Breeding:* small, keeled plate develops on upper mandible; pale yellow crest on back of head. *Nonbreeding* and *immature:* white plumage is tinged with brown.
Size: L 4½–6 ft; W 9 ft.
Voice: generally quiet; rarely issues piglike grunts.
Status: common in migration and as flocks of nonbreeding wanderers in summer on the eastern plains and western valleys.
Habitat: lakes, river mouths and marshes.

Similar Birds

Snow Goose
(p. 20)

Ross's Goose

short tail

black primary and
secondary wing
feathers

nonbreeding

very large, stocky,
white bird

naked orange skin
patch around eye

long, orange bill
and throat pouch

nonbreeding

Nesting: colonial; on a bare, low-lying island; nest scrape is unlined or is lined with twigs; dull white eggs are 3⅜ x 2¼ in; pair incubates 2 eggs for 29–36 days.

Did You Know?

The feathers on a pelican's wing tips are black and have a pigment called melanin that doesn't wear away in the wind.

Look For

When pelicans fly into the wind, they often stay close to the surface of the water. When the wind is at their backs, they will fly much higher.

Double-crested Cormorant

Phalacrocorax auritus

The Double-crested Cormorant looks like a bird but smells and swims like a fish. With a long, rudderlike tail and excellent underwater vision, this slick-feathered bird has mastered the underwater world. Most waterbirds have waterproof feathers, but the structure of the Double-crested Cormorant's feathers allows water in. "Wettable" feathers make this bird less buoyant, which in turn makes it a better diver. The Double-crested Cormorant also has sealed nostrils for diving, and therefore must fly with its bill open.

Other ID: all-black body; blue eyes. *Nonbreeding:* no plumes trail from eyebrow. *Immature:* brown upperparts; buff throat and breast; yellowish throat patch. *In flight:* rapid wingbeats; kinked neck.
Size: L 26–32 in; W 4¼ ft.
Voice: generally quiet; may issue pig-like grunts or croaks, especially near nest colonies.
Status: locally abundant summer resident on the eastern plains.
Habitat: large lakes and meandering rivers.

Similar Birds

Common Loon

Look For

Double-crested Cormorants often perch on trees or piers with their wings partially spread. Lacking oil glands, they use the sun and wind to dry their feathers.

fine plumes trail
from eyebrows

long, crooked
neck

thin bill,
hooked
at tip

orange-yellow
throat pouch

juvenile

breeding

Nesting: colonial; on an island or high in a
tree; platform nest is made of sticks and guano;
pale blue eggs are 2 x 1½ in; pair incubates
2–7 eggs for 25–30 days.

Did You Know?

Fish make up a large part of the Double-crested Cormorant's
diet, and this bird was previously thought to compete with
commercial and recreational fishermen for valued fish.
However, in natural environments, cormorants usually take
"undesireable" species, such as alewifes, smelts and yellow
perch.

Great Blue Heron
Ardea herodias

The long-legged Great Blue Heron has a stealthy, often motionless hunting strategy. It waits for a fish or frog to approach, spears the prey with its bill, then flips its catch into the air and swallows it whole. Herons usually hunt near water, but they also stalk fields and meadows in search of rodents.
• Great Blue Herons settle in communal treetop nests called "rookeries". Nesting herons are sensitive to human disturbance, so observe this bird's behavior from a distance.

Other ID: blue-gray overall; long, dark legs; dark crown. *Breeding:* richer colors; plumes streak from crown and throat. *In flight:* black upperwing tips; legs trail behind body; slow, steady wingbeats.
Size: L 4¼–4½ ft; W 6 ft.
Voice: quiet away from the nest; occasional harsh *frahnk frahnk frahnk* during takeoff.
Status: fairly common migrant and summer resident, primarily on the eastern plains; a few birds may overwinter.
Habitat: forages along the edges of rivers, lakes and marshes; also in fields and wet meadows.

Similar Birds

Little Blue Heron

Great Egret

Snowy Egret

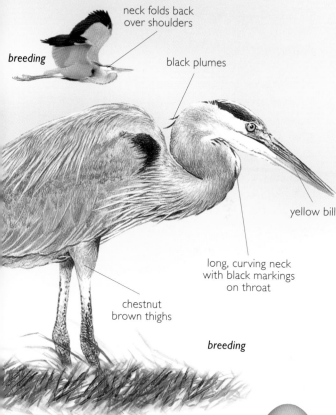

neck folds back over shoulders

breeding

black plumes

yellow bill

long, curving neck with black markings on throat

chestnut brown thighs

breeding

Nesting: colonial; adds to its stick platform nest over years; nest width can reach 4 ft; pale bluish green eggs are 2½ x 1¾ in; pair incubates 4–7 eggs for approximately 28 days.

Did You Know?

The Great Blue Heron is the tallest of all herons and egrets in North America.

Look For

In flight, the Great Blue Heron folds its neck back over its shoulders in an S-shape. Similar-looking cranes stretch their necks out when flying.

Cattle Egret
Bubulcus ibis

In overgrown agricultural fields, stoic groups of Cattle Egrets stare silently as people rush past in their cars. Over the last century—and without help from humans—the Cattle Egret has dispersed from Africa to inhabit pastureland and roadsides on every continent except Antarctica. These natural wanderers spread from Africa to Brazil, then, by the 1940s, to Florida and across the United States. • Cattle Egrets follow tractors or grazing animals, catching any insects that are stirred up. Invertebrates make up a main portion of their diet, whereas many other egrets eat mainly fish.

Other ID: *Breeding:* long plumes on throat and rump; purple lores. *Nonbreeding:* yellow-orange bill; black legs. *Immature:* similar to adult but with black feet and dark bill.
Size: L 19–21 in; W 35–37 in.
Voice: generally silent away from the breeding colony; most common call is an unmusical *rick-rack*.
Status: uncommon migrant on the eastern plains; increasingly locally common during summer.
Habitat: agricultural fields, abandoned lots, ranchlands and marshes.

Similar Birds

Great Egret

Snowy Egret

buff orange
crown, throat
and rump

orange-red
bill

mostly white
plumage

orange-red
legs

breeding

Nesting: colonial; often among other herons; in a tree or tall shrub; female builds a platform or shallow bowl with sticks supplied by the male; pale blue eggs are 1¾ x 1⅜ in; pair incubates 3–4 eggs for 21–26 days.

Did You Know?

This bird's scientific name *Bubulcus* means "belonging to or concerning cattle."

Look For

When foraging, the Cattle Egret sometimes uses a "leapfrog" feeding strategy, in which birds leap over one another, stirring up insects for the birds that follow.

Black-crowned Night-Heron

Nycticorax nycticorax

When dusk's long shadows shroud the marshes, Black-crowned Night-Herons arrive to hunt in the marshy waters. These herons crouch motionless, using their large, light-sensitive eyes to spot prey lurking in the shallows. • Black-crowned Night-Herons breed throughout much of the United States. Watch for them in summer, between dawn and dusk, as they fly from nesting colonies to feeding areas and back.

Other ID: black back; white foreneck and under-parts; gray neck and wings; dull yellow legs; stout, black bill. *Immature:* streaked with brown and white.
Size: *L* 23–26 in; W 3½ ft.
Voice: deep, guttural *quark* or *wok*, often heard as the bird takes flight.
Status: common migrant; local summer resident.
Habitat: shallow cattail and bulrush marshes, lakeshores and along slow rivers.

Similar Birds

Green Heron

American Bittern

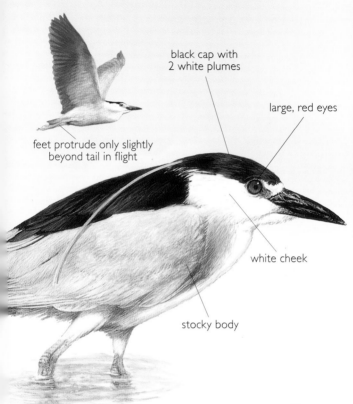

black cap with
2 white plumes

large, red eyes

feet protrude only slightly
beyond tail in flight

white cheek

stocky body

Nesting: colonial; in a tree or shrub; male gathers the nest material; female builds a loose nest platform of twigs and sticks and lines it with finer materials; pale green eggs are 2 x 1½ in; pair incubates 3–4 eggs for 21–26 days.

Did You Know?

Nycticorax, meaning "night raven," refers to this bird's distinctive nighttime calls.

Look For

To distinguish Black-crowned Night-Herons in flight, look at their feet, which are shorter than other herons and project only partially beyond the tail.

White-faced Ibis
Plegadis chihi

Ibises are slender, long-legged, highly social wading birds revered in many parts of the world. The White-faced Ibis is a bird of the larger wetlands of western North America and occupies the same habitats as the Glossy Ibis of eastern North America. Ibises require high-quality marshes for nesting and will abandon and relocate breeding sites to ensure optimal conditions. • In Colorado, localized breeding colonies are found mainly in the San Luis Valley, including up to 150 pairs at the Monte Vista and Alamosa national wildlife refuge colonies.

Other ID: dark red eyes. *Nonbreeding* and *immature:* generally brown with more indistinct greenish gloss; pinkish bare skin in front of eye; long, dark legs.
Size: L 19–26 in. W 36 in.
Voice: generally quiet; occasionally gives a series of low, ducklike quacks.
Status: fairly common migrant on the eastern plains; local summer resident.
Habitat: larger wetlands and marshes, flooded fields, wet meadows and marshy shorelines of lakes.

Similar Birds

Long-billed Curlew

Look For

The long legs, slender toes and remarkable downcurved bill help the White-faced Ibis extract invertebrates from soft or semifluid soil.

nonbreeding

eyes bordered by
white facial skin

rich red
facial patch

long, downcurved,
reddish olive bill

iridescent greenish lower
back and wing coverts

rich red legs   *breeding*

Nesting: colonial; in bulrushes or other emergent vegetation; deep cup nest of coarse materials is lined with fine plant matter; bluish green eggs are 2 x 1½ in; pair incubates 3–4 eggs for about 22 days.

Did You Know?

Ibises prefer flooded croplands and the expansive reed beds or muddy shallows of federal wildlife refuges. They fly rapidly, easily traversing the miles between secluded nesting colonies and outlying feeding locations.

Turkey Vulture
Cathartes aura

Turkey Vultures are intelligent, playful and social birds. Groups live and sleep together in large trees, or "roosts." Some roost sites are over a century old and have been used by the same family of vultures for several generations. • The genus name *Cathartes* means "cleanser" and refers to this bird's affinity for carrion. A vulture's bill and feet are much less powerful than those of eagles, hawks or falcons, which kill live prey. Its red, featherless head may appear grotesque, but this adaptation allows the bird to stay relatively clean while feeding on messy carcasses.

Other ID: *Immature:* gray head. *In flight:* head appears small; rocks from side to side when soaring.
Size: *L* 25–31 in; *W* 5½–6 ft.
Voice: generally silent; occasionally produces a hiss or grunt if threatened.
Status: common migrant at lower elevations; fairly common summer resident in the foothills.
Habitat: usually flies over open country, shorelines or roads; rarely over forests.

Similar Birds

Golden Eagle

Bald Eagle
(p. 60)

wings are held in a shallow "V"

silver gray flight feathers

bare, red head

brownish overall

pale, hooked bill

Nesting: in a cave, crevice, log or among boulders; uses no nest material; dull white or creamy, brown-spotted eggs are 2¾ x 2 in; pair incubates 2 eggs for up to 41 days.

Did You Know?

A threatened Turkey Vulture will play dead or throw up. The odor of its vomit repulses attackers, much like the odor of a skunk's spray does.

Look For

No other bird uses updrafts and thermals in flight as well as the Turkey Vulture. Pilots have reported seeing vultures soaring at 20,000 feet.

Bald Eagle

Haliaeetus leucocephalus

This majestic sea eagle hunts mostly fish and is often found near water. While soaring hundreds of feet high in the air, an eagle can spot fish swimming underwater and small rodents scurrying through the grass. Eagles also scavenge carrion and steal food from other birds. • Bald Eagles do not mature until their fourth or fifth year—only then do they develop the characteristic white head and tail plumage.

Other ID: *1st year:* dark overall; dark bill; some white in underwings. *2nd year:* dark "bib"; white in underwings. *3rd year:* mostly white plumage; yellow at base of bill; yellow eyes. *4th year:* light head with dark facial streak; variable pale and dark plumage; yellow bill; paler eyes.

Size: *L* 30–43 in; *W* 5½–8 ft.

Voice: thin, weak squeal or gull-like cackle: *kleek-kik-kik-kik* or *kah-kah-kah.*

Status: remains federally listed as threatened; increasing in numbers across Colorado in both summer and winter.

Habitat: large lakes and rivers.

Similar Birds

Golden Eagle

Osprey

white head and tail

yellow bill

immature

yellow feet

Nesting: increasing in Colorado; in a tree; usually, but not always, near water; huge stick nest is often reused for many years; white eggs are 2¾ x 2⅛ in; pair incubates 1–3 eggs for 34–36 days.

Did You Know?

The Bald Eagle, a symbol of freedom, longevity and strength, became the emblem of the United States in 1782.

Look For

In winter, hundreds of ducks will gather on ice-free waters, unknowingly providing an easy meal for as many as 800 Bald Eagles wintering in Colorado.

Red-tailed Hawk
Buteo jamaicensis

Take an afternoon drive through the country and look for Red-tailed Hawks soaring above the fields. Red-tails are the most common hawks in Colorado, especially in winter. • In warm weather, these hawks use thermals and updrafts to soar. The pockets of rising air provide substantial lift, which allows migrating hawks to fly for almost 2 miles at a time without flapping their wings. On cooler days, resident Red-tails perch on exposed tree limbs, fence posts or utility poles to scan for prey.

Other ID: brown eyes. *In flight:* light underwing flight feathers with faint barring; dark leading edge on underside of wing.
Size: *Male:* L 18–23 in; W 4–5 ft. *Female:* L 20–25 in; W 4–5 ft.
Voice: powerful, descending scream: *keeearrrr.*
Status: fairly common migrant and year-round resident.
Habitat: open country with some trees; also roadsides or woodlots.

Similar Birds

Rough-legged Hawk

Swainson's Hawk

Ferruginous Hawk (p. 64)

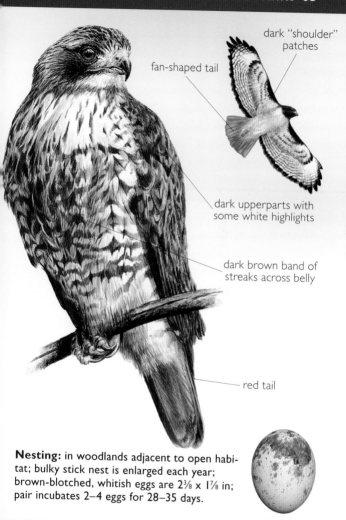

dark "shoulder" patches

fan-shaped tail

dark upperparts with some white highlights

dark brown band of streaks across belly

red tail

Nesting: in woodlands adjacent to open habitat; bulky stick nest is enlarged each year; brown-blotched, whitish eggs are 2⅜ x 1⅞ in; pair incubates 2–4 eggs for 28–35 days.

Did You Know?

The Red-tailed Hawk's piercing call is often paired with the image of an eagle in TV commercials and movies.

Look For

Courting Red-tails will sometimes dive at one another, lock talons and tumble toward the earth, breaking away at the last second to avoid crashing into the ground.

Ferruginous Hawk

Buteo regalis

A favorite among birders, the regal Ferruginous Hawk inhabits open grasslands and deserts. East of the Rocky Mountains, this large, richly colored hawk often lives in close association with ground squirrels and prairie-dogs, and small groups of birds often perch near prairie-dog colonies, waiting to surprise their prey. • Lately, conservationists have been concerned about this species' numbers. Conversion of native grasslands to agricultural lands as well as rodent control campaigns have reduced and localized the range of Ferruginous Hawks. These birds are currently listed as threatened in several states and as a species of special concern in Canada.

Other ID: largest buteo hawk. *Dark morph:* dark underparts; white tail; dark wing linings; light flight feathers. *Immature:* very light; might have light-colored legs.
Size: *L* 23 in; *W* 4½ ft.
Voice: typical, hawk-style *kreeah,* dropping at the end.
Status: state-listed as a species of special concern; uncommon breeder in summer; fairly common in winter on the eastern plains, uncommon in the west.
Habitat: open grasslands, low riparian areas and croplands.

Similar Birds

Red-tailed Hawk
(p. 62)

Swainson's Hawk

Rough-legged Hawk

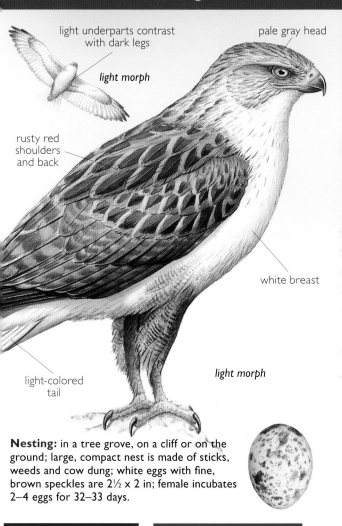

light underparts contrast with dark legs

light morph

pale gray head

rusty red shoulders and back

white breast

light-colored tail

light morph

Nesting: in a tree grove, on a cliff or on the ground; large, compact nest is made of sticks, weeds and cow dung; white eggs with fine, brown speckles are 2½ x 2 in; female incubates 2–4 eggs for 32–33 days.

Did You Know?

Approximately one-fifth of the Ferruginous Hawks wintering in the United States are found in Colorado.

Look For

Light-morph adults have nearly white underparts and hold their rufous legs in a distinctive "V" in flight.

American Kestrel
Falco sparverius

The colorful American Kestrel, formerly known as the "Sparrow Hawk," is a common and widespread falcon, not shy of human activity and adaptable to habitat change. This small falcon has benefited from the grassy rights-of-way created by interstate highways, which provide habitat for grasshoppers and other small prey. Watch for this robin-sized bird along rural roadways, perched on poles and telephone wires, or hovering over agricultural fields, foraging for insects and small mammals.

Other ID: lightly spotted underparts. *In flight:* long, rusty tail; frequently hovers; buoyant, indirect flight style.
Size: L 7½–8 in; W 20–24 in.
Voice: usually silent; loud, often repeated, shrill *killy-killy-killy* when excited; female's voice is lower pitched.
Status: common year-round at lower elevations.
Habitat: open fields, riparian woodlands, woodlots, forest edges, bogs, roadside ditches, grassy highway medians, grasslands and croplands.

Similar Birds

Merlin

Sharp-shinned Hawk

Peregrine Falcon

2 distinctive facial stripes

blue-gray crown with rusty cap

♂

♀

rusty barring on back

♂

rusty wings and breast streaking

blue-gray wings

Nesting: in a tree cavity; may use a nest box; white to buff, brown-spotted eggs are 1½ x 1⅛ in; mostly the female incubates 4–6 eggs for 29–30 days; pair raises the young together.

Did You Know?

No stranger to captivity, the American Kestrel was the first falcon to reproduce by artificial insemination.

Look For

The American Kestrel repeatedly lifts its tail while perched to scout below for prey.

Prairie Falcon
Falco mexicanus

Rocketing overhead like a fighter jet, the Prairie Falcon often seems to appear out of nowhere. This western raptor of arid openlands is best identified by its brown plumage and dark "wing pits." • In spring and summer, Prairie Falcons often concentrate their hunting efforts on ground squirrel colonies, swooping over windswept grass to pick off naive youngsters. As summer fades to fall, large flocks of migrating songbirds often capture the attention of these pallid "ghosts of the plains."

Other ID: *In flight:* pointed wings; long, narrow, banded tail; quick wingbeats and direct flight.
Size: *Male:* L 14–15 in; W 3–3¼ ft. *Female:* L 17–18 in; W 3¼–3½ ft.
Voice: generally silent; alarm call near nest is a rapid, shrill *kik-kik-kik-kik.*
Status: uncommon year-round resident, more common at higher elevations in summer.
Habitat: *Breeding:* river canyons, cliffs, rimrocks or rocky promontories in arid, open lowlands or high intermontane valleys. *In migration* and *winter:* open, treeless country, such as fields, pastures and sagebrush flats.

Similar Birds

Peregrine Falcon

American Kestrel
(p. 66)

pale face with dark brown cap and nape

white patch behind eye

brown upperparts

narrow, brown "mustache" stripe

diagnostic dark "wing pits"

white underparts with brown spotting

Nesting: on a cliff ledge or in a crevice; rarely in an abandoned crow or raptor nest; usually without nest material; brown-spotted, whitish eggs are 2 x 1½ in; mostly the female incubates 3–5 eggs for about 30 days.

Did You Know?

Newly fledged falcons risk serious injury or death in early hunting forays, sometimes misjudging their flight speed or their ability to pull out of a dive.

Look For

Prairie Falcons commonly soar for long periods on updrafts and along ridgelines or perch on the crossbar of utility poles.

American Coot
Fulica americana

American Coots resemble ducks but are actually more closely related to rails and gallinules. Good numbers of coots appear on our lakes, reservoirs and wetlands from May to September. During the breeding season, they are aggressively territorial and constantly squabble with other water-birds in their space. You might catch a glimpse of a coot scooting across the water, flailing its wings and splashing an opponent. • With feet that have individually webbed toes, the coot is well adapted to div-ing, but it isn't afraid to snatch a meal from another skilled diver.

Other ID: red eyes; long, yellow-green legs; lobed toes; small, white marks on tail.
Size: *L* 13–16 in; *W* 24 in.
Voice: calls frequently in summer, day and night: *kuk-kuk-kuk-kuk-kuk;* also croaks and grunts.
Status: common migrant and summer resident in the west; rare local resident in winter.
Habitat: shallow marshes, ponds and wetlands with open water and emer-gent vegetation; also sewage lagoons.

Similar Birds

Pied-billed Grebe

Surf Scoter

Black Scoter

reddish spot on white forehead shield

gray-black overall

white, chicken-like bill with dark ring around tip

Nesting: in emergent vegetation; pair builds a floating nest of cattails and grass; buffy white, brown-spotted eggs are 2 x 1⅜ in; pair incubates 8–12 eggs for 21–25 days; usually raises 2 broods.

Did You Know?

American Coots are the most widespread and abundant members of the rail family in North America.

Look For

Many features distinguish a coot from a duck, including head bobbing while swimming or walking and a narrower bill that extends up the forehead.

Sandhill Crane
Grus canadensis

Each spring and fall, thousands of Sandhill Cranes gather in Colorado's San Luis Valley, a major stop-over point on their migration route. Peak migration counts may reach 17,000 cranes, which stop to forage in the mudflats and nearby fields before continuing on their journey. Every year in late February, the Monte Vista National Wildlife Refuge hosts a festival to encourage better understanding and appreciation for cranes and other wildlife. • The Sandhill Crane's deep, rattling call can be heard long before this bird passes overhead. Its coiled trachea alters the pitch of its voice, making its call sound louder and carry farther.

Other ID: long, straight bill; long neck; dark legs.
Size: L 3¼–4¼ ft; W 6–7 ft.
Voice: loud, resonant, rattling: *gu-rrroo gu-rrroo gurrroo.*
Status: abundant in migration in the San Luis Valley; irregular migrant elsewhere.
Habitat: *Breeding:* isolated, open marshes, fens and bogs lined with trees or shrubs. *In migration:* agricultural fields and shorelines.

Similar Birds

Great Blue Heron
(p. 50)

Whooping Crane

naked, red crown

white cheek and chin

gray plumage is often stained rusty red from iron oxides in the water

Nesting: rare nester in the northern mountains; in the water or along a shoreline; on a large mound of aquatic vegetation; brown-blotched, buff eggs are 3¾ x 2⅜ in; pair incubates 2 eggs for 29–32 days.

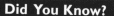

Did You Know?

Cranes mate for life and reinforce pair bonds each spring with an elaborate courtship dance that looks much like human dancing.

Look For

Large, V-shaped flocks of Sandhill Cranes look like flocks of Canada Geese, but the cranes often soar and circle higher in the air, and they do not honk like geese.

Killdeer

Charadrius vociferus

The Killdeer is a gifted actor, well known for its "broken wing" distraction display. When an intruder wanders too close to its nest, the Killdeer greets the interloper with piteous cries while dragging a wing and stumbling about as if injured. Most predators take the bait and follow, and once the Killdeer has lured the predator far away from its nest, it miraculously recovers from the injury and flies off with a loud call.

Other ID: brown head; white neck band; brown back and upperwings; white underparts; rufous rump. *Immature:* downy; only 1 breast band.
Size: L 9–11 in; W 24 in.
Voice: loud, distinctive *kill-dee kill-dee kill-deer;* variations include *deer-deer.*
Status: fairly common migrant and summer resident, except at the highest elevations.
Habitat: open areas, such as fields, lakeshores, sandy beaches, mudflats, gravel streambeds, wet meadows and grasslands.

Similar Birds

Semipalmated Plover

Piping Plover

Mountain Plover

black forehead band

white eyebrow and patch above bill

2 black breast bands

long, pinkish legs

Nesting: on open ground, in a shallow, usually unlined depression; heavily marked, creamy buff eggs are 1⅜ x 1⅛ in; pair incubates 4 eggs for 24–28 days; may raise 2 broods.

Did You Know?

In spring, you might hear a European Starling imitate the vocal Killdeer's call.

Look For

The Killdeer has adapted well to urbanization, and it finds golf courses, farms, fields and abandoned industrial areas as much to its liking as shorelines.

American Avocet
Recurvirostra americana

An American Avocet in full breeding plumage is a sight to remember: its peachy red head and neck, needlelike bill and bold black and white body paint an elegant picture against the uniform mudflats. • Avocets nest on the shorelines of low-elevation, alkaline lakes and wetlands in valleys, including North Park, the San Luis Valley and, more recently, near Grand Junction. Females have been known to parasatize the nests of other avocets and perhaps other species. Conversely, avocets have incubated Common Tern and Black-necked Stilt eggs, raising the adopted chicks along with their own young.

Other ID: white underparts. *Female:* has a more upturned, shorter bill than the male. *Nonbreeding:* gray head, neck and breast. *In flight:* long, skinny legs and neck; black and white wings.
Size: L 17–18 in; W 31 in.
Voice: harsh, shrill *plee-eek plee-eek.*
Status: fairly common migrant on the eastern plains and western valleys; local summer resident.
Habitat: *Breeding:* lakeshores, alkaline wetlands and exposed mudflats. *In migration:* reservoirs and lakeshores.

Similar Birds

Black-necked Stilt

Willet

Marbled Godwit

breeding

black wings with wide, white patches

long, upturned, black bill

peachy red head, neck and breast

long, pale blue legs

♂

breeding

Nesting: semicolonial; along a dried mudflat, always near water; pair builds a shallow scrape or a mound of vegetation lined with debris; darkly blotched, buff eggs are 2 x 1½ in; pair incubates 4 eggs for 23–25 days.

Did You Know?

The American Avocet can issue a specialized, rising alarm call that simulates the Doppler effect and gives the impression of quickly moving closer.

Look For

The American Avocet is the only avocet in the world that undergoes a yearly color change. Its peach-colored breeding hood changes to gray in winter.

Spotted Sandpiper
Actitis macularius

The female Spotted Sandpiper, unlike most other female birds, lays her eggs and leaves the male to tend the clutch. She diligently defends her territory and may mate with several different males. Only about one percent of birds display this unusual breeding strategy known as "polyandry." Each summer, the female can lay up to four clutches and is capable of producing 20 eggs. As the season progresses, however, available males become harder to find. Come August, there may be seven females for every available male.

Other ID: teeters almost continuously *Nonbreeding* and *immature:* pure white breast and throat; brown bill; dull yellow legs. *In flight:* flies close to the water's surface with very rapid, shallow wingbeats.
Size: *L* 7–8 in; *W* 15 in.
Voice: sharp, crisp *eat-wheat, eat-wheat, wheat-wheat-wheat-wheat.*
Status: fairly common migrant statewide; fairly common summer resident in western Colorado; uncommon summer resident on the eastern plains.
Habitat: shorelines, gravel beaches, drainage ditches, swamps and sewage lagoons; occasionally seen in cultivated fields.

Similar Birds

Solitary Sandpiper

Dunlin

long tail

white eyebrow

dark eye line

breeding

short, white upper wing stripe

white underparts are heavily spotted with black

yellow-orange legs

breeding

Nesting: usually near water; sheltered by vegetation; shallow scrape is lined with grass; darkly blotched, creamy buff eggs are 1¼ x 1 in; male incubates 4 eggs for 20–24 days.

Did You Know?

Sandpipers have four toes: three pointing forward and one pointing backward. Plovers, such as the Killdeer, have only three toes.

Look For

Spotted Sandpipers bob their tails constantly on shore and fly with rapid, shallow, stiff-winged strokes.

Lesser Yellowlegs
Tringa flavipes

The "tattletale" Lesser Yellowlegs is the self-appointed sentinel in a mixed flock of shorebirds, raising alarm at the first sign of a threat. • It is challenging to discern Lesser Yellowlegs and Greater Yellowlegs in the field, but with practice, you will notice that the Lesser's bill is finer, straighter and shorter—about as long as its head is wide. With its long legs and wings, the Lesser appears slimmer than the Greater, and it is more commonly seen in flocks. Finally, the Lesser Yellowlegs emits a pair of peeps, whereas the Greater Yellowlegs peeps three times.

Other ID: subtle, dark eye line; pale lores.
Nonbreeding: grayer overall.
Size: L 10–11 in; W 24 in.
Voice: typically a high-pitched pair of *tew* notes; noisiest on breeding grounds.
Status: common migrant on the eastern plains and western valleys.
Habitat: shorelines of lakes, rivers, marshes and ponds.

Similar Birds

Willet

Greater Yellowlegs

Solitary Sandpiper

brown-black mottling on upperparts

all-dark bill is not noticeably longer than width of head

lacks barring on belly

bright yellow legs

breeding

Nesting: does not nest in Colorado; nests in the Arctic; in open muskeg or a natural forest opening; in a depression on a dry mound lined with leaves and grass; darkly blotched, buff to olive eggs are 1⅝ x 1⅛ in; pair incubates 4 eggs for 22–23 days.

Did You Know?

Yellowlegs were popular game birds in the 1800s because they were plentiful and easy to shoot.

Look For

When feeding, the Lesser Yellowlegs wades into water almost to its belly, sweeping its bill back and forth just below the water's surface.

Wilson's Phalarope
Phalaropus tricolor

Phalaropes are the wind-up toys of the bird world: they spin and whirl about in tight circles, stirring up the water. Then, with their needlelike bills, they help themselves to the aquatic insects and small crustaceans that funnel toward the surface.

• Phalaropes are "polyandrous," meaning that a female phalarope mates with several males. She abandons each mate after egg laying and leaves him to incubate the eggs and tend the young while she seeks out other males to mate with.

Other ID: dark, needlelike bill; white eyebrow and throat; light underparts; black legs. *Breeding female:* very sharp colors. *Breeding male:* duller overall. *Nonbreeding:* all-gray upperparts; white eyebrow; gray cap and eye line; dark yellowish or greenish legs.
Size: L 8½–9½ in; W 17 in.
Voice: deep, grunting *work work* or *wu wu wu,* usually given on the breeding grounds.
Status: common migrant; locally fairly common summer resident.
Habitat: *Breeding:* marshes, wet meadows and margins of sewage lagoons. *In migration:* also lakeshores.

Similar Birds

Red-necked Phalarope

Look For

Unlike most birds, the female phalarope is more colorful than the male. The male phalarope's dull colors help camouflage him while he incubates the eggs.

brown cap and
eye line

pale chestnut
sides of neck

black eye line extends
down side of neck
and onto back

gray cap

♂

♀

chestnut brown
sides of neck

breeding

Nesting: often near water; well concealed
in a depression lined with vegetation; brown-
blotched, buff eggs are 1½ x 1 in; male incubates
4 eggs for 18–27 days and rears the young.

Did You Know?

While incubating eggs, the male phalarope sheds the feathers
on his belly and develops a thick skin on his underside. This
"brood patch" swells with blood and provides the right temperature for incubation. In most other species, the female
develops the brood patch.

Franklin's Gull
Larus pipixcan

The Franklin's Gull is not a typical "seagull." This land-loving bird spends much of its life inland and nests on the prairies, where it is affectionately known as "Prairie Dove." It often follows tractors across agricultural fields, snatching up insects from the tractor's path in much the same way its cousins follow fishing boats. • Franklin's Gull is one of only two gull species that migrate long distances between breeding and wintering grounds—the majority of Franklin's Gulls overwinter along the Pacific coasts of Peru and Chile.

Other ID: gray mantle; white underparts.
Breeding: black head; red-orange bill and legs; breast often has pinkish tinge.
Size: L 13–15 in; W 3 ft.
Voice: shrill, "mewing" *weeeh-ah weeeh-ah* while feeding and in migration; also a shrill *kuk-kuk-kuk.*
Status: common in migration, especially in fall; wandering nonbreeding flocks may be present in summer.
Habitat: agricultural fields, marshy lakes, landfills and large river and lake shorelines.

Similar Birds

Bonaparte's Gull   Common Tern   Forster's Tern
(p. 90)

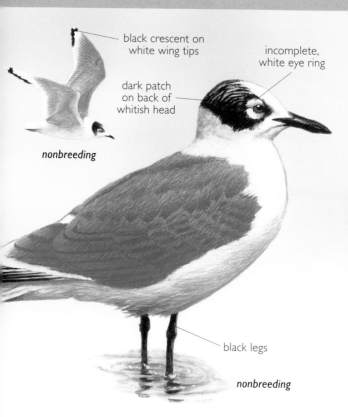

black crescent on white wing tips

incomplete, white eye ring

dark patch on back of whitish head

nonbreeding

nonbreeding

black legs

Nesting: doesn't breed in Colorado; breeds in the northern Great Plains and Canadian prairies; colonial; usually in dense emergent vegetation; floating platform nest is built above water; variably marked, pale greenish or buff eggs are 2 x 1⅜ in; pair incubates 2–3 eggs for 23–26 days.

Did You Know?

This gull was named for Sir John Franklin, the British navigator and explorer who led four expeditions to the Canadian Arctic in the 19th century.

Look For

Big flocks of these gulls may linger on our large lakes and rivers during fall migration. In spring, smaller flocks move through to breeding grounds more quickly.

Ring-billed Gull

Larus delawarensis

Few people can claim that they have never seen this common and widespread gull. Highly tolerant of humans, Ring-billed Gulls are part of our everyday lives, scavenging our litter and frequenting our parks. These omnivorous gulls eat almost anything and swarm parks, beaches, golf courses and fast-food parking lots looking for food handouts, making pests of themselves. However, few species have adjusted to human development as well as the Ring-billed Gull, which is something to appreciate.

Other ID: *Breeding:* white head. *In flight:* black wing tips with a few white spots.
Size: *L* 18–20 in; *W* 4 ft.
Voice: high-pitched *kakakaka-akakaka;* also a low, "laughing" *yook-yook-yook.*
Status: abundant migrant and winter resident on the eastern plains; uncommon nonbreeding summer resident.
Habitat: *Summer:* bare, rocky and shrubby islands and sewage ponds. *In migration* and *winter:* lakes, rivers, landfills, golf courses, fields and parks.

Similar Birds

Herring Gull

California Gull

nonbreeding

white head

black ring
around bill tip

yellow eyes

pale gray
mantle

white
underparts

yellow legs

nonbreeding

Nesting: does not breed in Colorado; nests in the northern U.S. and Canada; colonial; in a shallow scrape on the ground lined with grass, debris and small sticks; brown-blotched, gray to olive eggs are 2⅜ x 1⅝ in; pair incubates 2–4 eggs for 23–28 days.

Did You Know?

In chaotic nesting colonies, adult Ring-billed Gulls will call out and can recognize the response of their chicks.

Look For

To differentiate between gulls, pay attention to the markings on their bills and the color of their eyes and legs.

Black Tern
Chlidonias niger

Black Terns rule the skies above cattail marshes. These acrobatic birds wheel about in feeding flights, picking minnows from the water's surface and catching insects in midair. • Wetland habitat loss and degradation have caused Black Tern populations to decline. These birds are sensitive nesters and will not return to a nesting area if the water level or plant density changes. Wetland conservation efforts may eventually help these birds recover to their former abundance.

Other ID: *Breeding:* gray back, wings and tail; reddish black legs. *Nonbreeding:* white underparts and forehead; molting fall birds may be mottled with brown.
In flight: long, pointed wings; shallowly forked tail.
Size: L 9–10 in; W 24 in.
Voice: greeting call is a shrill, metallic *kik-kik-kik-kik-kik*; typical alarm call is *kreea*.
Status: common migrant on the eastern plains; uncommon local summer resident.
Habitat: shallow marshes, wet meadows, lake edges and sewage ponds with emergent vegetation.

Similar Birds

Forster's Tern
(p. 90)

Common Tern

nonbreeding

black head and
underparts

black bill

black bill

white undertail
coverts

breeding

Nesting: loosely colonial; flimsy nest of dead plant material is built on floating vegetation, a muddy mound or a muskrat house; darkly blotched, olive to pale buff eggs are 1⅜ x 1 in; pair incubates 3 eggs for 21–22 days.

Did You Know?

The Black Tern's genus name is a variation of *chelidonias*, the Greek word for "swallow." The name reflects the tern's darting, swallowlike flight pattern.

Look For

Flocks of Black Terns can be seen snatching insects from the air at dawn and dusk.

Forster's Tern
Sterna forsteri

The Forster's Tern so closely resembles the Common Tern that the two often seem indistinguishable to the eyes of many observers. Only when these terns acquire their distinctive fall plumages do birders begin to note the Forster's presence.

• Forster's Tern has an exclusively North American breeding distribution, but it bears the name of a man who never visited this continent: German naturalist Johann Reinhold Forster (1729–98). Forster, who lived and worked in England, examined tern specimens sent from Hudson Bay, Canada. He was the first to recognize this bird as a distinct species.

Other ID: pure white underparts. *Breeding:* light gray mantle; white rump. *Nonbreeding:* lacks black cap; black band through eyes; black bill. *In flight:* forked, gray tail; long, pointed wings.
Size: L 14–16 in; W 31 in.
Voice: flight call is a nasal, short *keer keer;* also a grating *tzaap.*
Status: fairly common migrant on the eastern plains; uncommon local summer resident.
Habitat: freshwater lakes, rivers and marshes.

Similar Birds

Common Tern

Franklin's Gull
(p. 84)

nonbreeding

large, orange, black-tipped bill.

black cap and nape

long, gray tail with white outer edges

orange legs

breeding

Nesting: occasionally colonial; on a platform of floating vegetation in a freshwater or saltwater marsh; olive to buff, blotched eggs are 1⅝ x 1¼ in; pair incubates 2–3 eggs for 24 days.

Did You Know?

This tern's bill color changes from black in winter to orange with a black tip in summer.

Look For

Like most terns, the Forster's Tern catches fish in dramatic headfirst dives, but it also snatches flying insects in midair.

Rock Pigeon
Columba livia

Rock Pigeons are familiar to most anyone who has lived in the city. These colorful, acrobatic, seed-eating birds frequent parks, town squares, railroad yards and factory sites. Their tolerance of humans has made them a source of entertainment, as well as a pest. • This pigeon is likely a descendant of a Eurasian bird that was first domesticated about 4500 BC. The Rock Pigeon was introduced to North America in the 17th century by settlers.

Other ID: *In flight:* holds wings in a deep "V" while gliding; white rump on most birds.
Size: *L* 12–13 in; *W* 28 in (male is usually larger).
Voice: soft, cooing *coorrr-coorrr-coorrr.*
Status: common year-round resident except at the highest elevations.
Habitat: urban areas, railroad yards and agricultural areas; high cliffs often provide more natural habitat.

Similar Birds

Mourning Dove
(p. 96)

Band-tailed Pigeon
(p. 94)

color is highly variable
(iridescent blue-gray,
red, white or tan)

white
cere

usually has
orange feet

Nesting: in a barn or on a cliff, bridge or
tower; in a flimsy nest of sticks, grass and other
vegetation; glossy white eggs are 1½ x 1⅛ in;
pair incubates 2 eggs for 16–19 days; may raise
broods year-round.

Did You Know?

Both Caesar and
Napoleon used Rock
Pigeons as message
couriers.

Look For

No other "wild" bird varies
as much in coloration, a
result of semidomestication
and extensive inbreeding
over time.

Band-tailed Pigeon
Patagioenas fasciata

Though similar in size, form and behavior to the familiar Rock Pigeon, the Band-tailed Pigeon has a distinctive white crescent on its nape as well as a unique yellow bill and yellow legs. Through much of its range in the Americas, the Band-tailed Pigeon inhabits foothills and lower mountains.

• Suburban backyards adjacent to stands of tall trees support their share of Band-tailed Pigeons, but these birds also inhabit more secluded forests. They feed by plucking at nuts and fruits while clinging clumsily to twigs that may scarcely support their weight.

Other ID: overall plumage in varying shades of gray; dark eye; purplish head and breast. *In flight:* pale underparts; long tail.
Size: L 13–15 in; W 26 in.
Voice: generally quite silent; very deep, *Ooh, uh-WOO*.
Status: fairly common locally in south-western and south-central Colorado during summer.
Habitat: ponderosa pine or oak woodlands and adjacent farmland or riparian areas.

Similar Birds

Rock Pigeon
(p. 92)

Mourning Dove
(p. 96)

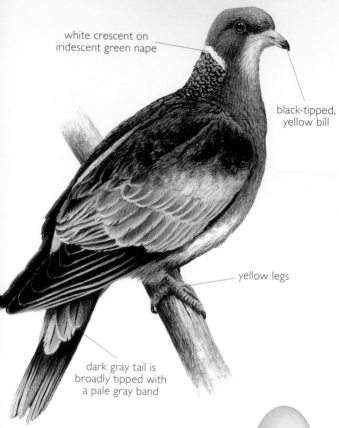

white crescent on iridescent green nape

black-tipped, yellow bill

yellow legs

dark gray tail is broadly tipped with a pale gray band

Nesting: on a forked branch; fragile platform of sticks with minimal lining; white egg is 1⅝ x 1⅛ in; pair incubates a single egg for 18–20 days; young are fed "pigeon milk."

Did You Know?

A heavy slapping of broad wings may reveal this bird's presence high within the canopy.

Look For

Band-tailed Pigeons are fond of acorns and are generally most numerous in forests with a strong oak component.

Mourning Dove
Zenaida macroura

The Mourning Dove's soft cooing, which filters through broken woodlands and suburban parks, is often confused with the sound of a hooting owl. Beginning birders who track down the source of the calls are often surprised to find the stream-lined silhouette of a perched dove. • This popular game animal is common throughout Colorado and is one of the most abundant native birds in North America. Its numbers and range have increased since human development created more open habitats and food sources, such as waste grain and bird feeders.

Other ID: buffy, gray-brown plumage; small head; dark bill; sleek body; dull red legs.
Size: L 11–13 in; W 18 in.
Voice: mournful, soft, slow *oh-woe-woe-woe*.
Status: abundant migrant and summer resident at lower elevations; rare in winter.
Habitat: open and riparian woodlands, forest edges, agricultural and suburban areas, open parks.

Similar Birds

Rock Pigeon
(p. 92)

Yellow-billed Cuckoo

pale blue eye ring

dark, shiny patch below ear

pale rosy underparts

long, white-trimmed, tapering tail

black spots on upperwing

Nesting: in a shrub or tree; occasionally on the ground; nest is a fragile, shallow platform of twigs; white eggs are 1⅛ x ⅞ in; pair incubates 2 eggs for 14 days.

Did You Know?

The Mourning Dove raises up to six broods each year—more than any other native bird.

Look For

When the Mourning Dove bursts into flight, its wings clap above and below its body. It also often creates a whistling sound as it flies at high speed.

Western Screech-Owl

Megascops kennicottii

Like many of the smaller owls, the Western Screech-Owl is a fierce and adaptable hunter, often adding birds larger than itself to its usual diet of insects, amphibians and small mammals. This chunky, open-woodland owl passes the daylight hours concealed in dense shrubs or roosting in a hollow tree. • Between March and June, the distinctive "bouncing-ball" courting whistles indicate the presence of a pair of Western Screech-Owls.

Other ID: grayish overall.
Size: *Male: L* 8–9 in; *W* 18–20 in. *Female: L* 10–11 in; *W* 22–24 in.
Voice: courtship song is series of soft, accelerating, even-pitched whistles, with a rhythm like that of a bouncing ball coming to a stop; also gives a short trill followed by a longer trill; pairs often harmonize.
Status: fairly common year-round resident in the southeastern foothills; uncommon year-round resident in the western valleys.

Habitat: mid-elevation forests of all types, including coniferous forests with juniper stands, chaparral and oak woodlands, riparian woodlands, towns, orchards, farms and ranches.

Similar Birds

Flammulated Owl

Eastern Screech-Owl
(p. 100)

Northern Saw-whet
Owl (p. 106)

yellow eyes

often shows small "ear" tufts

partially dark-bordered facial disc

gray bill

narrow, dark, vertical breast stripes

Nesting: in an abandoned woodpecker cavity, stump, nest box or magpie nest; adds no nest material; white eggs are 1½ x 1¼ in; female incubates 2–5 eggs for about 26 days.

Did You Know?

Robert Kennicott, for whom this species is named, traveled and collected owl specimens across northern Canada and Alaska in the mid-1800s.

Look For

Western Screech-Owls are primarily found south of the South Platte River, whereas most Eastern Screech-Owls are found north of the Arkansas River.

Eastern Screech-Owl
Megascops asio

The diminutive Eastern Screech-Owl is a year-round resident of low-elevation, deciduous woodlands, but its presence is rarely detected—most screech-owls sleep away the daylight hours. • The noise of a mobbing horde of chickadees or a squawking gang of Blue Jays can alert you to an owl's presence during the day. Smaller birds that mob a screech-owl often do so after losing a family member during the night. • Unique among Colorado owls, Eastern Screech-Owls show both red and gray color morphs. In Colorado, the gray morph is more common, with only one red morph on record. Very rarely, an intermediate brown morph occurs.

Other ID: yellow eyes; pale grayish bill. *Red morph: reddish overall.*
Size: *L* 8–9 in; *W* 20–22 in.
Voice: horselike "whinny" that rises and falls.
Status: fairly common year-round resident in the northeastern plains.
Habitat: mature deciduous forests, open deciduous and riparian woodlands, orchards and shade trees with natural cavities.

Similar Birds

Northern Saw-whet Owl (p. 106)

Flammulated Owl

Western Screech-Owl (p. 98)

short "ear" tufts

grayish overall

dark breast streaking

gray morph

Nesting: in an unlined natural cavity or artificial nest box; white eggs are 1½ x 1¼ in; female incubates 4–5 eggs for about 26 days; male brings food to the female during incubation.

Did You Know?

The adaptable screech-owl has one of the most varied diets of any owl. It will capture small animals, earthworms, insects and even fish.

Look For

Eastern Screech-Owls are well adapted to the presence of people—they may use human-made nest boxes and they may even bathe in suburban birdbaths.

Great Horned Owl
Bubo virginianus

This highly adaptable and superbly camouflaged hunter has sharp hearing and powerful vision that allow it to hunt at night as well as by day. It will swoop down from a perch onto almost any small creature that moves. • An owl has specially designed feathers on its wings to reduce noise. The leading edge of the flight feathers is fringed rather than smooth, which interrupts airflow over the wing and allows the owl to fly noiselessly. • Great Horned Owls begin their courtship as early as January, and by February and March the females are already incubating their eggs.

Other ID: overall plumage varies from light gray to dark brown; heavily mottled, gray, brown and black upperparts; yellow eyes; white chin.

Size: L 18–25 in; W 3–5 ft.

Voice: breeding call is 4–6 deep hoots: *hoo-hoo-hoooo hoo-hoo* or *Who's awake? Me too*; female gives higher-pitched hoots.

Status: fairly common year-round resident at lower elevations; less common at higher elevations.

Habitat: fragmented forests, fields, riparian woodlands, suburban parks and wooded edges of landfills.

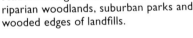

Similar Birds

Long-eared Owl

Look For

Owls regurgitate pellets that contain the indigestible parts of their prey. You can find these pellets, which are generally clean and dry, under frequently used perches.

tall, widely spaced "ear" tufts form a triangle with bill

rusty orange facial disc is outlined in black

fine, horizontal barring on breast

Nesting: in another bird's abandoned stick nest or in a tree cavity; adds little or no nest material; dull whitish eggs are 2¼ x 1⅞ in; mostly the female incubates 2–3 eggs for 28–35 days.

Did You Know?

A Great Horned Owl's eyes are fixed, unable to move in their sockets the way a human's eyes can. Nonetheless, this owl is able to look in any direction it wants—its flexible neck can turn 180 degrees to the left or right. In contrast to its acute vision, this owl has a poor sense of smell, which might explain why it is the only consistent predator of skunks!

Burrowing Owl
Athene cunicularia

The Burrowing Owl is a loyal inhabitant of the prairies. Its favorite haunts are heavily grazed pastures in intensively cultivated regions and disturbed areas in extensive grasslands. It nests in an underground burrow abandoned by another animal, and the extermination of ground squirrels in the prairies has greatly reduced the number of suitable owl nest sites. Collisions with vehicles, the effect of agricultural chemicals and the conversion of native grasslands to cropland are thought to be some of the other challenges facing this threatened bird.

Other ID: long legs; short tail; rounded head; yellow bill. *Immature:* brownish band across breast; pale, unbarred underparts.

Size: *L* 9–11 in; *W* 21–24 in.

Voice: call is a harsh *chuk*; chattering *quick-quick-quick*; rattlesnake-like warning call when inside its burrow. *Male: coo-hooo* courtship call.

Status: state-listed as threatened; declining populations in Colorado; fairly common in summer on the eastern plains; occasional winter sightings.

Habitat: open, short-grass haylands, pastures and prairies; occasionally on lawns and golf courses.

Similar Birds

Short-eared Owl

Northern Saw-whet Owl (p. 106)

white around eyes

brown upperparts are flecked with white

bold, white chin stripe

horizontal barring on underparts

Nesting: singly or in loose colonies; in an abandoned natural or artificial burrow; nest is lined with bits of dry manure, food debris, feathers and fine grass; white eggs are 1¼ x 1 in; female incubates 5–11 eggs for 27–30 days.

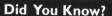

Did You Know?

The Burrowing Owl's range and population numbers have decreased drastically in recent years.

Look For

During the day, these owls perch on top of fence posts or at the entrance to their burrows, where they look very similar to ground squirrels.

Northern Saw-whet Owl
Aegolius acadicus

The tiny Northern Saw-whet Owl makes the most of every hunting opportunity. When temperatures fall below freezing and prey is abundant, the saw-whet will catch more than it can eat. It usually stores the extra food in trees and allows it to freeze. When hunting efforts fail, the hungry owl returns to thaw out the frozen cache, "incubating" the food as if it were a clutch of eggs! The saw-whet's favorite foods include mice, voles, large insects and songbirds.

Other ID: large, rounded head; dark bill; short tail. *Juvenile:* white patch between eyes; rich brown head and breast; buff brown belly.
Size: L 7–9 in; W 16–18 in.
Voice: whistled, evenly spaced *whew-whew*, repeated about 100 times per minute.
Status: fairly common year-round resident in the foothills and lower mountains.
Habitat: coniferous and mixed forests; wooded city parks and ravines.

Similar Birds

Boreal Owl

Western Screech-Owl
(p. 98)

buffy facial disc

white spots on wings

brown streaking on belly

Nesting: in a natural tree hollow or a nest box; white eggs are 1¼ x 1 in; female incubates 5–6 eggs for 27–29 days; male feeds the female during incubation.

Did You Know?

This owl's name refers to its call, which sounds like a saw blade being sharpened. The call can also be compared to the "bleeping" sound of a vehicle reversing.

Look For

One way to detect the Northern Saw-whet Owl is by looking for "whitewash," or buildup of excrement, under roosting sites.

Common Nighthawk
Chordeiles minor

The Common Nighthawk makes an unforgettable booming sound as it flies high overhead. In an energetic courting display, the male dives, then swerves skyward, making a hollow *vroom* sound with its wings. • Like other members of the nightjar family, the Common Nighthawk is well adapted to catch insects in midair: its large, gaping mouth is surrounded by feather shafts that funnel insects into its bill. A nighthawk can eat over 2600 insects in one day, including mosquitoes, blackflies and flying ants. • Look for nighthawks foraging for insects at nighttime baseball games.

Other ID: *Male:* white throat. *Female:* buff throat. *In flight:* shallowly forked, barred tail; erratic flight.
Size: L 8–10 in; W 23–26 in.
Voice: frequently repeated, nasal *peent peent;* wings make a deep, hollow *vroom* during a courtship dive.
Status: fairly common summer resident, except at higher elevations.
Habitat: *Breeding:* forest openings, bogs, rocky outcroppings and gravel rooftops. *In migration:* often near water; any area with large numbers of flying insects.

Similar Birds

Common Poorwill

Look For

With their short legs and tiny feet, nighthawks sit lengthwise on tree branches and blend in perfectly with the bark.

bold, white "wrist" patches on long, pointed wings

very small bill

cryptic, mottled plumage

♂

barred underparts

Nesting: on bare ground; no nest is built; heavily marked, creamy white to buff eggs are 1⅛ x ⅞ in; female incubates 2 eggs for about 19 days; pair feeds the young together.

Did You Know?

Despite its name, the Common Nighthawk is generally less nocturnal than other nightjars. It is most active at dawn and dusk and often forages on the insects attracted to streetlights. Nightjars spend most of the daylight hours resting on tree limbs or on the ground.

White-throated Swift
Aeronautes saxatalis

This avian marvel certainly earned its wings as a true aeronaut—the generic name *aeronautes* means "sky sailor." Only brief, cliff-clinging rest periods and annual nesting duties keep it grounded—the White-throated Swift feeds, drinks, bathes and even mates while flying. • Relatively common in the mountainous areas and even in some cities in the western United States, these birds live up to their family name. Swifts have been clocked at up to 200 miles per hour—fast enough to avoid the talons of hungry Prairie Falcons.

Other ID: small, slender, aerial insectivore; dark upperparts; white-tipped secondaries.
Size: L 6–7 in. W 15 in.
Voice: loud, shrill, descending *skee-jee-ee-ee-ee-ee-ee.*
Status: common summer resident in the foothills.
Habitat: *Breeding:* high cliffs and crags in open country, especially dry escarpments surrounded by coniferous forest, high desert fault blocks and river canyons; ranges widely in search of food. *In migration:* more likely at lower elevations.

Similar Birds

Chimney Swift

Black Swift

Tree Swallow

long, tapering wings
are angled backward

sides of rump
are white

white throat, tapering to
undertail coverts

long, thin, slightly
forked tail

Nesting: gathers nest material on the wing;
cup nest of soft materials glued together with
saliva is attached to a cliff, bridge or building;
white or creamy eggs are ⅞ x ⁹⁄₁₆ in; pair incubates 4–5 eggs for 24 days.

Did You Know?

During its lifetime, the average White-throated Swift
is likely to travel more than
a million miles—enough to
take it around the world
more than 40 times!

Look For

White-throats are easily rec-
ognized by their loud, sharp,
scraping notes, black-and-
white coloring and rapid,
rather erratic flight.

Black-chinned Hummingbird

Archilochus alexandri

Black-chinned Hummingbirds are habitat generalists that occur in a variety of sites throughout their range, from arid deserts to lush residential areas. In Colorado, they are mainly found in the western valleys, especially in pinyon-juniper shrublands and riparian areas. • Taxonomist H.G.L. Reichenbach was deeply influenced by Greek mythology and named this hummingbird after Archilochus, a notable Greek poet.

Other ID: small, white crescent behind eye; iridescent green upperparts; long, thin bill. *Female* and *immature:* white throat may have faint gray or greenish streaks; pale underparts often have grayish sides.
Size: L 3–3½ in; W 4¾ in.
Voice: soft, high-pitched, warbling courtship songs; buzz and *chip* alarm calls; males' wings buzz in flight.
Status: fairly common summer resident in the southwestern valleys; uncommon summer resident farther north and east.
Habitat: lowland riparian woodlands, orchards and shrub-filled canyons; wanderers may feed in gardens.

Similar Birds

Calliope Hummingbird

Broad-tailed Hummingbird (p. 114)

Rufous Hummingbird (p. 116)

white underparts with a dull green "vest"

black throat with an iridescent violet band

♂

flat, gray forehead

black eye line

♀

buff tinge on flanks

Nesting: tiny cup nest of plant down and spiderwebs is saddled atop a branch; white eggs are ½ x ¼ in; female incubates 2 eggs for up to 16 days.

Did You Know?

Nectar-rich native wildflowers or a feeder stocked with a solution of 4 parts water and 1 part sugar will attract hummingbirds to your yard.

Look For

The dark purple and black markings on the male's head often make him appear black-headed.

Broad-tailed Hummingbird

Selasphorus platycercus

Best known for the metallic trill produced by the male's wings, the Broad-tailed Hummingbird is often heard before it is seen. It breeds during the short montane flowering season and conserves energy during food shortages or cool nights by lowering its respiration rate and body temperature. • These hummingbirds breed in the foothills and mountainous regions of the western U.S. and overwinter in Mexico. During summer and migration, they frequent coniferous forests, flowering mountain meadows and suburban areas throughout the western half of Colorado.

Other ID: *Male:* dark tail. *Female:* dark streaking on cheeks and throat; buffy sides; broad, dark tail with rufous base and white tips.
Size: L 4 in; W 5¼ in.
Voice: high *chip* notes; male's wings produce a unique, metallic trill in flight.
Status: fairly common migrant and summer resident to the timberline in western Colorado.
Habitat: subalpine meadows and montane forests, especially pine-oak or pinyon pine woodlands; often near streams; also gardens.

Similar Birds

Rufous Hummingbird
(p. 116)

Calliope
Hummingbird

Black-chinned
Hummingbird (p. 112)

long, straight bill

bright, iridescent green
crown and back

rosy red throat

green and buffy wash
to white underparts

♂

Nesting: nest hangs from a branch, often over a stream; female builds a cup nest of plant material, spiderwebs and lichen or bark; white eggs are ½ x ⅜ in; female incubates 2 eggs for 14–17 days; may raise 2 broods.

Did You Know?

While most hummingbirds survive three to five years in the wild, one female Broad-tailed Hummingbird lived a record 12 years.

Look For

Males perform dramatic aerial courtship displays that include a sequence of impressive climbs and dives, accompanied by a distinct wing trill.

Rufous Hummingbird
Selasphorus rufus

The tiny Rufous Hummingbird is a delicate avian jewel, but its beauty hides a relentless mean streak. Sit patiently in a flower-filled meadow or alongside a hummingbird feeder, and you'll soon notice the aggressiveness of these feisty birds. They buzz past one another and chase rivals for some distances.

• Hummingbirds are among the few birds that are able to fly vertically and in reverse. In forward flight, they beat their wings up to 80 times per second, and their hearts can beat up to 1200 times per minute!

Other ID: mostly rufous tail. *Male:* iridescent, orange-red throat; orangy brown back, tail and flanks; some adult males have green backs. *Female:* may have red-spotted throat.

Size: *L* 3–3½ in; W 4½ in.

Voice: call is a low *chewp chewp*; also utters a rapid and exuberant confrontation call, *ZEE-chuppity-chup!*

Status: common summer and early fall migrant to the timberline in the west.

Habitat: nearly any habitat with abundant flowers, including gardens; edges of coniferous and deciduous forests; burned sites; brushy slopes and alpine meadows.

Similar Birds

Calliope
Hummingbird

Black-chinned
Hummingbird (p. 112)

Broad-tailed
Hummingbird (p. 114)

long, thin, black bill

green back

♂

♀

white breast
and belly

rufous sides and
flanks contrast with
white underparts

Nesting: doesn't breed in Colorado; breeds in northwestern North America; in a tree or shrub; tiny cup nest of plant down, bark fragments and spider silk is covered with lichens; white eggs are ½ x ⅜ in; female incubates 2 eggs for 15–17 days; young fledge at 21 days.

Did You Know?

Weighing about as much as a nickel, hummingbirds are capable of flying at speeds up to 60 miles per hour.

Look For

Extremely aggressive, the Rufous Hummingbird will defend a feeder from all other species.

Red-headed Woodpecker

Melanerpes erythrocephalus

This bird of the East lives mostly in open deciduous woodlands, urban parks and oak savannas.
Red-heads were once common throughout their
range, but their numbers have declined dramati-
cally over the past century. Since the introduction
of the European Starling, Red-headed Woodpeckers have been largely outcompeted for nesting
cavities. • These birds are frequent traffic fatalities,
often struck by vehicles when they dart from their
perches and over roadways to catch flying insects.

Other ID: white underparts; black tail. *Juvenile:* brown back,
wings and tail; slight brown streaking on white underparts.
Size: L 9–9½ in; W 17 in.
Voice: loud series of *kweer* or *kwrring* notes; occasionally
a chattering *kerr-r-ruck*; also drums softly
in short bursts.
Status: fairly common migrant and
summer resident on the eastern plains.
Habitat: open deciduous woodlands
(especially oak woodlands), urban
parks, river edges and roadsides with
groves of scattered trees.

Similar Birds

Red-bellied
Woodpecker

Lewis's Woodpecker

Red-naped Sapsucker
(p. 120)

bright red head

black back
and wings

white lower back

brown head

juvenile

large, white
patch

Nesting: male excavates a nest cavity in a dead tree or limb; white eggs are 1 x ¾ in; pair incubates 4–5 eggs for 12–13 days; pair feeds the young together.

Did You Know?

The Red-headed Woodpecker is one of only four woodpecker species that regularly caches food.

Look For

The forested bottomlands, swamps and semi-open habitats of Colorado are favorite haunts of this charismatic bird.

Red-naped Sapsucker

Sphyrapicus nuchalis

The Red-naped Sapsucker is an inconspicuous woodpecker that drills shallow holes in the bark of trees, then returns later to eat the insects and oozing sap. This deliberate foraging practice has convinced some people that this bird is capable of planning. • Sapsuckers don't actually suck sap; they lap it up with a long tongue that resembles a frayed paintbrush. • Some people worry that the activities of this sapsucker will kill ornamental trees and shrubs, but most healthy plants can withstand a series of sapsucker wells.

Other ID: yellow wash on breast; white rump; light yellow upper back with fine black streaking. *Female:* white chin; red throat. *In flight:* obvious white upperwing patch not on trailing edge.
Size: L 8½ in; W 16 in.
Voice: call is catlike *meow*; tapping is irregular like morse code.
Status: fairly common summer resident in the foothills and lower mountains.
Habitat: *Breeding:* variety of deciduous and mixed forests, especially with aspen, birch or alder; montane riparian stands, clearings and burns. *In migration:* lower-elevation riparian woodlands, orchards, tree groves and shade trees.

Similar Birds

Williamson's
Sapsucker

Lewis's Woodpecker

Hairy Woodpecker

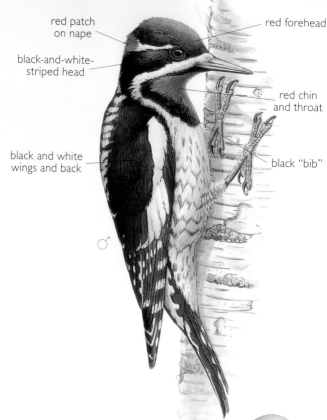

red patch on nape

black-and-white-striped head

black and white wings and back

red forehead

red chin and throat

black "bib"

♂

Nesting: pair excavates a cavity in a living or rotting aspen or birch; occasionally uses the same tree for 2 years, making a new hole; cavity is lined with wood chips; white eggs are ⅞ x ⅝ in; pair incubates 4–5 eggs for 13 days.

Did You Know?

Abandoned sapsucker nest cavities are often occupied by other animals, including northern flying squirrels and many bird species.

Look For

Lines of parallel "wells" drilled in the bark of living trees, especially conifers and trembling aspens, are a sure sign that a sapsucker has visited your area.

Downy Woodpecker
Picoides pubescens

A pair of Downy Woodpeckers at your backyard bird feeder will brighten a frosty winter day. These approachable little birds are more tolerant of human activity than most other species, and they visit feeders more often than the larger, more aggressive Hairy Woodpeckers. • Like other wood-peckers, the Downy has evolved special features to help cushion the shock of repeated hammering, including a strong bill and neck muscles, a flexible, reinforced skull and a brain that is tightly packed in its protective cranium.

Other ID: black eye line and crown; white patch on back; white belly. *Male:* small, red patch on back of head. *Female:* no red patch.
Size: L 6–7 in; W 12 in.
Voice: long, unbroken trill; calls are a sharp *pik* or *ki-ki-ki* or whiny *queek queek*.
Status: uncommon year-round resident, except at the highest elevations.
Habitat: any wooded environment, especially deciduous and mixed forests and areas with tall, deciduous shrubs.

Similar Birds

Hairy Woodpecker

Yellow-bellied Sapsucker

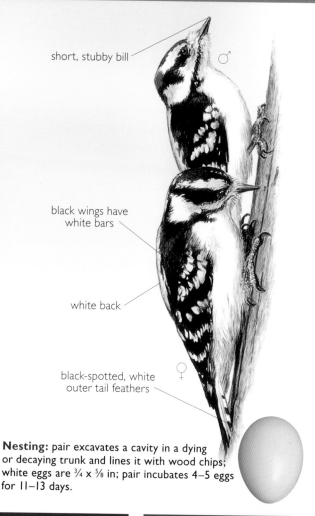

short, stubby bill ♂

black wings have white bars

white back

black-spotted, white outer tail feathers ♀

Nesting: pair excavates a cavity in a dying or decaying trunk and lines it with wood chips; white eggs are ¾ x ⅝ in; pair incubates 4–5 eggs for 11–13 days.

Did You Know?

Woodpeckers have feathered nostrils, which filter out the sawdust produced by hammering.

Look For

Both Downy Woodpeckers and Hairy Woodpeckers have white outer tail feathers, but the Downy's have several dark spots whereas the Hairy's are pure white.

Northern Flicker
Colaptes auratus

Instead of boring holes in trees, the Northern Flicker scours the ground in search of invertebrates, particularly ants. With robinlike hops, it investigates anthills, grassy meadows and forest clearings. • To clean itself, a flicker will occasionally squash ants and preen itself with the remains. Ants contain formic acid, which kills small parasites on the bird's skin and feathers. • Both red-shafted and yellow-shafted forms of this species occur in Colorado. The yellow-shafted form occurs primarily in the eastern plains, whereas the red-shafted form occurs across the state but is more common in the west. Intergrades may occur where both forms are present.

Other ID: long bill; brownish gray face; brown crown; white rump. *Male:* red "mustache" stripe. *Female:* no "mustache."
Size: *L* 12–13 in; *W* 20 in.
Voice: loud, "laughing," rapid *kick-kick-kick-kick-kick-kick; woika-woika-woika* issued during courtship.
Status: fairly common year-round resident, except at the highest elevations.
Habitat: *Breeding:* open woodlands and forest edges, fields, meadows, beaver ponds and other wetlands. *In migration* and *winter:* urban gardens and woodlots.

Similar Birds

Red-bellied Woodpecker

Red-naped Sapsucker (p. 120)

Ladder-backed Woodpecker

black "bib"

♂

brown, black-barred back and wings

black-spotted buff to whitish underparts

♀

"Red-shafted Flicker"

Nesting: pair excavates a cavity in a dying or decaying trunk and lines it with wood chips; may also use a nest box; white eggs are 1⅛ x ⅞ in; pair incubates 5–8 eggs for 11–16 days.

Did You Know?

The very long tongue of a woodpecker wraps around twin structures in the skull and is stored like a measuring tape in its case.

Look For

Flickers often bathe in dusty depressions. The dust particles absorb oils and bacteria that can harm the birds' feathers.

Western Wood-Pewee

Contopus sordidulus

Aspiring birders will quickly come to recognize the burry, down-slurred call of the Western Wood-Pewee as one of the most common summertime noises in woodlands of western Colorado. • Though it breeds mainly in aspen forests, the Western Wood-Pewee also frequents edge habitats, riparian areas and open pine woodlands. • Overall, numbers of Western Wood-Pewees appear to be declining. Loss or alteration of riparian habitat through clear-cutting or grazing and the destruction of tropical rain forests are likely contributing factors.

Other ID: pale throat; dark lower mandible; light undertail coverts.
Size: *L* 5–6 in; *W* 10½ in.
Voice: plaintive whistle, *purREER*; song is *oom-VLIVVIT... purREER*.
Status: common migrant and summer resident in the foothills and lower mountains.
Habitat: most semi-open forest habitats including cottonwood riparian, ponderosa pine and montane conifer or mixed woodlands.

Similar Birds

Olive-sided Flycatcher

Willow Flycatcher

Dusky Flycatcher
(p. 128)

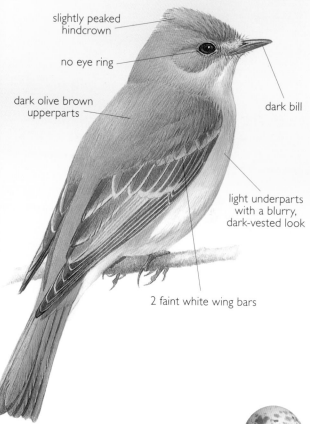

slightly peaked hindcrown

no eye ring

dark olive brown upperparts

dark bill

light underparts with a blurry, dark-vested look

2 faint white wing bars

Nesting: on a horizontal limb in a tree; female builds a small cup nest of plant fibers bound with spider silk; brown-spotted, whitish eggs are ¹¹⁄₁₆ x ⁹⁄₁₆ in; female incubates 3 eggs for 12–13 days.

Did You Know?

The scientific descriptor *sordidulus* refers to the Western Wood-Pewee's dusky, "dirty" color.

Look For

Wood-Pewees launch themselves into aerobatic, looping foraging ventures in search of flying insects, often returning immediately to the same perch.

Dusky Flycatcher
Empidonax oberholseri

The Dusky Flycatcher is one of seven species of *Empidonax* flycatchers that are regularly found in Colorado. The "empids" are among the most challenging birds to identify, and many individuals cannot be identified specifically. Vocalizations are key to distinguishing these species, so readers of this book are advised to document any non-singing migrants that pass through our state as "*Empidonax* species." • The scientific name *oberholseri* honors Dr. Harry Oberholser, one of the finest 20th-century ornithologists. He worked for the U.S. Fish and Wildlife Service and the Cleveland Natural History Museum.

Other ID: olive brown upperparts; dark bill with orange at base of lower mandible; white throat.
Size: *L* 5–6 in; *W* 8¼ in.
Voice: male's call is a quick, whistled *PREE-tick-preet*, rising at the end.
Status: common migrant and summer resident in western Colorado.
Habitat: *Breeding:* montane chaparral, sapling-dotted forest openings, brushy montane meadows. *In migration:* a variety of open woodland habitats, riparian woodlands and chaparral.

Similar Birds

Hammond's Flycatcher

Willow Flycatcher

Cordilleran Flycatcher

rounded head

light-colored eye ring

short wings

2 faint white wing bars

long, dark tail trimmed with white

Nesting: in the fork of a small shrub; small cup nest of plant material, feathers and fur; creamy or pale yellow, speckled eggs are ⅝ x ½ in; female incubates 3–4 eggs for 15–16 days.

Did You Know?

The Dusky Flycatcher was once considered a subspecies of the Gray Flycatcher but was given a distinct status based on DNA analysis, behavior and habitat.

Look For

Empidonax flycatchers are small birds that often flip up their tails.

Say's Phoebe
Sayornis saya

Partial to dry environments, the Say's Phoebe thrives in sun-parched grassy valleys, hot, dry canyons and ranchlands. Abandoned buildings provide a secure, sheltered nest site that can be reused every year, and livestock conveniently stir up insects that the Phoebe "hawks" from a fence post or other low perch. • This is the only bird whose genus and species names are derived from the same person, Thomas Say. A versatile naturalist, his primary contributions were in the field of entomology.

Other ID: dark tail; brown-gray breast and upperparts; very faint wing bars; constantly bobs its tail.
Size: L 7½ in; W 13 in.
Voice: song is *pitseedar;* call is a softly whistled *pee-ur.*
Status: fairly common summer resident in the foothills and mesas; locally uncommon summer resident in the eastern plains.
Habitat: hot, dry canyons, ravines, rimrocks, valleys and gullies dominated by grasses and shrubs; may also use agricultural areas and scrublands.

Similar Birds

American Robin, female (p. 172)

Look For

This bird flycatches and gleans buildings, vegetation or streamsides for insects. Sometimes it runs short distances in pursuit of prey.

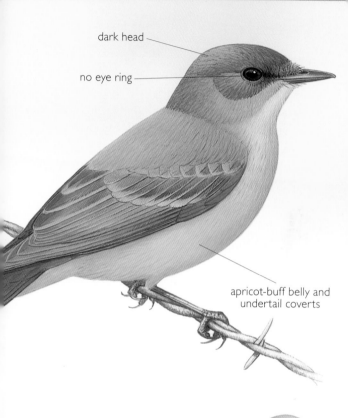

dark head

no eye ring

apricot-buff belly and
undertail coverts

Nesting: in a niche on a cliff face, beneath an eave or bridge; nest of grass, moss and fur; white, usually unmarked eggs are ¾ x ⁹⁄₁₆ in; female incubates 4–5 eggs for up to 17 days.

Did You Know?

Flycatchers have bills that are generally fairly broad and flat. The wider bill provides a greater surface area in which the prey can be caught, increasing the chance that when the fly-catcher's bill snaps shut, at least some part of the insect will be caught in its grasp.

Western Kingbird
Tyrannus verticalis

Kingbirds are a group of flycatchers that perch on wires or fence posts in open habitats. They passionately guard their territories, fearlessly chasing out larger birds. Once you have witnessed a kingbird's brave attacks against much larger birds, such as crows and hawks, you'll understand why this rabble-rouser was awarded its regal common name.

• The tumbling aerial courtship display of the Western Kingbird is a good indication that this bird might be breeding. The male twists and turns as he rises to heights of 65 feet above the ground, stalls, then tumbles and flips his way back to the earth.

Other ID: black bill; faint, dark gray mask; thin, orange crown (rarely seen); pale gray breast; black tail; white edges on outer tail feathers.

Size: L 8–9 in; W 15½ in.

Voice: chatty, twittering *whit-ker-whit*; also a short *kit* or extended *kit-kit-keetle-dot*.

Status: common summer resident in lower elevations; uncommon summer resident at higher elevations.

Habitat: open, dry country; grassy areas with scattered brush or hedgerows; edges of open fields; riparian woodlands.

Similar Birds

Cassin's Kingbird

Eastern Kingbird

Ash-throated Flycatcher

pale gray head

ashy gray wing coverts

whitish throat

yellow belly and undertail coverts

Nesting: in a deciduous tree or on a utility pole; bulky cup nest of grass and twigs is lined with soft material; whitish, heavily blotched eggs are ⅞ x ⅝ in; female incubates 3–5 eggs for 18–19 days.

Did You Know?

The scientific descriptor *verticalis* refers to the bird's hidden orange crown patch, which is flared during courtship displays and in combat with rivals.

Look For

A kingbird may chase an insect for up to 50 feet before finally capturing it.

Loggerhead Shrike

Lanius ludovicianus

The Loggerhead Shrike is truly in a class of its own. This predatory songbird has very acute vision, and it often perches atop trees and on wires to scan its surroundings for small prey, which is caught in fast, direct flight or a swooping dive. • Males display their hunting prowess by impaling prey on thorns or barbed wire. This behavior may also serve as a means of storing excess food during times of plenty. • Many shrikes become traffic fatalities when they fly low across roads to prey on insects attracted to the warm pavement.

Other ID: gray crown and back; white underparts.
In flight: white wing patches; white-edged tail.
Juvenile: brownish gray, barred upperparts.
Size: *L* 9 in; *W* 12 in.
Voice: *Male:* high-pitched, hiccupy *bird-ee bird-ee* in summer; infrequently a harsh *shack-shack* year-round.
Status: fairly common migrant at lower elevations; fairly common summer resident in the western valleys; uncommon summer resident in the eastern plains.
Habitat: grazed pastures and marginal and abandoned farmlands with scattered hawthorn shrubs, fence posts, barbed wire and nearby wetlands.

Similar Birds

Northern Shrike

Northern
Mockingbird (p. 174)

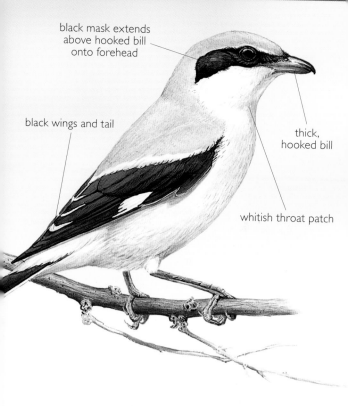

black mask extends above hooked bill onto forehead

black wings and tail

thick, hooked bill

whitish throat patch

Nesting: low in a shrub or small tree; bulky cup nest of twigs and grass is lined with animal hair, feathers and plant down; pale eggs with dark spots are 1 x ¾ in; female incubates 5–6 eggs for 15–17 days.

Did You Know?

Habitat loss has contributed to a steady decline in Loggerhead Shrike populations across North America.

Look For

Shrikes typically perch at the top of tall trees to survey the surrounding area for prey.

Warbling Vireo
Vireo gilvus

The Warbling Vireo is a common summer resident of the foothills and mountains of western Colorado. This vireo often settles close to urban areas, and by May its bubbly voice, uncharacteristic of vireos, may be heard in local parks, backyards and farmlands. Because the Warbling Vireo lacks any splashy field marks, it is undetectable unless it moves from one leaf-hidden stage to another.

• Population trends for this vireo are not well understood and vary geographically. In California, Warbling Vireo numbers have declined over the last two decades, whereas populations in eastern Canada have increased.

Other ID: white to pale gray underparts; brighter adults may have yellowish sides. *In flight:* broad-winged; drab above and white below.

Size: L 5–5½ in; W 8–9 in.

Voice: male's song is a long, musical warble of slurred whistles; catlike calls, 2-sylla-bled notes and a short, dry *gwit*.

Status: fairly common summer resident except at high elevations.

Habitat: deciduous forests and riparian woodlands; urban parks, orchards and farmlands.

Similar Birds

Red-eyed Vireo

Plumbeous Vireo

Orange-crowned Warbler

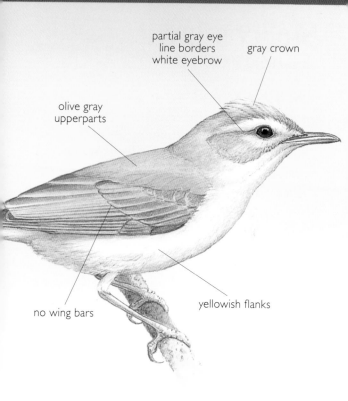

partial gray eye line borders white eyebrow

gray crown

olive gray upperparts

no wing bars

yellowish flanks

Nesting: in a horizontal fork of a tree or shrub; hanging basketlike cup nest of grass, roots, plant down and spider's silk; dark-spotted, white eggs are ¾ x ⁹⁄₁₆ in; pair incubates 4 eggs for 12 days.

Did You Know?

This bird breeds throughout much of North America, the broadest breeding range among our vireos.

Look For

Some Warbling Vireos are brighter with more yellow in their plumage, especially in fall.

Steller's Jay
Cyanocitta stelleri

With a dark crest and velvet blue feathers, the
stunning Steller's Jay is a resident jewel in our
foothills and lower mountains. Generally noisy
and pugnacious, this bird suddenly becomes
silent and cleverly elusive when nesting. • Bold
Steller's Jays will not hesitate to steal food scraps
from inattentive picnickers and scatter smaller
birds at feeders. • When Georg Wilhelm Steller,
the first European naturalist to visit Alaska, saw
his first Steller's Jay, its similarity to paintings of
the Blue Jay convinced him that he had arrived in
North America.

Other ID: *In flight:* grayish underwings with blue linings;
round-tipped blue tail; makes short glides.
Size: L 11–12 in; W 19 in.
Voice: harsh, far-carrying *shack-shack-
shack*; a grating *kresh, kresh.*
Status: fairly common year-round resident in the foothills and lower mountains.
Habitat: coniferous forests and pine-
oak woodlands to elevations of 8500 ft,
occasionally higher; townsites and
exotic tree plantations.

Similar Birds

Western Scrub-Jay

Gray Jay

Pinyon Jay
(p. 140)

bluish forehead streaks

large, black crest

black head, nape and back

glossy, deep velvet blue plumage

barred wings and tail

Nesting: in the fork of a conifer; bulky, stick-and-twig nest is lined with mud, grass and conifer needles; brown-marked, pale greenish blue eggs are 1¼ x ⅞ in; female incubates 4 eggs for 16 days.

Did You Know?

The range of the Steller's Jay includes the Rocky Mountains to the West Coast. The similar-looking Blue Jay lives east of the Rockies.

Look For

The Steller's Jay raises its long, black crest in confrontation with other birds.

Pinyon Jay

Gymnorhinus cyanocephalus

Loud, social Pinyon Jays are seed-caching birds found primarily in the pine forests of the foothills. When not breeding, these jays wander in sometimes enormous flocks that consist of many smaller family groups. • This bird's sharp bill allows it to open pine cones and remove the seeds; its specialized jaws absorb the force of heavy pounding. • One bird can carry up to 40 whole, unhulled pine seeds in its expandable esophagus (a Western Scrub-Jay can carry only five), and will bury them in traditional caching grounds. Individuals can accurately locate the hidden stores months later, even under snow.

Other ID: light streaks on throat; often flies in flocks.
Size: *L* 9–11½ in; *W* 19 in.
Voice: flight call is high, piercing *mew* or "laughing," repeated *hah-hah*; warning call is a low *krawk-krawk-krawk*.
Status: locally common year-round resident in the southwestern foothills; numbers fluctuate widely depending on food availability.
Habitat: *Breeding:* dry, open ponderosa pine, limber pine and juniper forest. *Foraging:* sagebrush flats, forests of pine and tall sagebrush.

Similar Birds

Steller's Jay
(p. 138)

Clark's Nutcracker
(p. 142)

Western Scrub-Jay

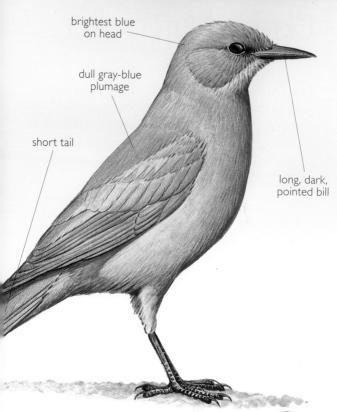

brightest blue on head

dull gray-blue plumage

short tail

long, dark, pointed bill

Nesting: in loose colonies; in pines, junipers and shrubs; pair builds a large, bulky nest of twigs and fibers; brown-marked, blue-green eggs are 1¼ x ⅞ in; female incubates 4–5 eggs for up to 17 days.

Did You Know?

Gymnorhinus means "naked nose" and refers to this bird's more exposed nostrils, which are an adaptation to keep facial feathers free of pine pitch.

Look For

In Colorado, where pinyon pine is absent, Pinyon Jays are found primarily in ponderosa pine, limber pine and juniper.

Clark's Nutcracker
Nucifraga columbiana

The Clark's Nutcracker has a long, sturdy bill for prying apart the cones of whitebark pine and other conifers, and a special throat pouch for transporting the seeds to carefully selected storage spots. These caches might be 8 miles or more apart, and together they may contain more than 30,000 seeds. Over winter and throughout the nesting cycle, nutcrackers use their phenomenal memory to relocate cache sites. • The whitebark pine is entirely dependent on the Clark's Nutcracker for seed dispersal, while the nutcracker relies on the pine's energy-rich seeds to successfully raise its young.

Other ID: whitish face; white undertail coverts.
In flight: stoops and tumbles unerringly along upper slopes of tall peaks.
Size: L 12–13 in; W 24 in.
Voice: loud, unpleasant, grating *kra-a-a-a-a,* delivered mostly from a perch.
Status: fairly common year-round resident in the mountains.
Habitat: *Breeding:* upper-elevation conifer forest; may use lower-elevation limber pine forest. *Winter:* may move to lower elevations.

Similar Birds

Gray Jay

Northern
Mockingbird (p. 174)

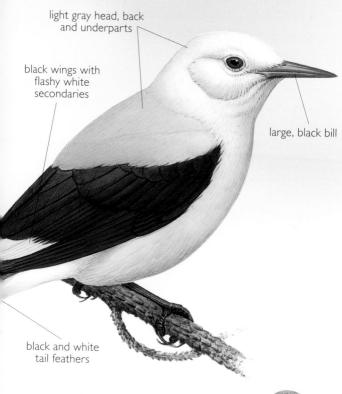

light gray head, back and underparts

black wings with flashy white secondaries

large, black bill

black and white tail feathers

Nesting: on a horizontal conifer limb; pair builds a stick platform nest lined with grass and strips of bark; darkly marked, greenish eggs are 1¼ x ⅞ in; pair incubates 2–4 eggs for 16–22 days.

Did You Know?

William Clark of the Lewis and Clark expedition mistook this bird for a woodpecker and placed it in the genus *Picicorvus*, or "woodpecker-crow."

Look For

Raucous and extroverted Clark's Nutcrackers are often encountered in campgrounds and picnic areas, looking to scavenge a meal.

Black-billed Magpie
Pica hudsonia

Truly among North America's most beautiful birds, Black-billed Magpies are too often discredited because of their aggressive demeanor. Whereas many westerners consider magpies a nuisance, eastern visitors to Colorado are often captivated by their beauty and approachability. • The magpie is one of the most exceptional architects among birds. The domed compartment of the nest conceals and protects eggs and young from harsh weather and predators. Abandoned nests remain in trees for years and are often reused by other birds.

Other ID: black head, breast and back; white belly; black undertail coverts. *In flight:* rounded, black and white wings.
Size: *L* 18 in; *W* 25 in.
Voice: loud, nasal, frequently repeated *ueh-ueh-ueh;* also many other vocalizations.
Status: common year-round resident in the mountains and the eastern plains.
Habitat: open forests, agricultural areas, riparian thickets, townsites and campgrounds.

Similar Birds

American Crow

Common Raven
(p. 146)

large, black bill

white wing patch

iridescent wings and
very long tail may
appear black

Nesting: in a tree or tall shrub; domed stick
and twig nest is often held together with mud;
brown-spotted, greenish gray eggs are 1¼ x 1 in;
female incubates 5–8 eggs for up to 24 days.

Did You Know?

Magpies raised in captivity
may learn how to imitate
the human voice and
"count" or distinguish
different-sized groups of
objects.

Look For

Albino magpies occasionally
occur. They have white bel-
lies and light gray, instead of
black, body feathers.

Common Raven
Corvus corax

The Common Raven soars with a wingspan comparable to that of a hawk's, traveling along coastlines, over deserts, along mountain ridges and even on the arctic tundra. Few birds occupy such a large natural range. • When bison roamed the prairies, Common Ravens were year-round residents in the Great Plains. Their numbers declined with the slaughter of the great bison herds, but recent reports suggest that these birds have begun to recolonize parts of their former range.

Other ID: all-black plumage; heavy, black bill; rounded wings.
Size: L 21–23 in; W 4 ft.
Voice: deep, guttural, far-carrying, repetitive *craww-craww* or *quork quork* among other vocalizations.
Status: common year-round resident, except in the eastern plains.
Habitat: coniferous and mixed forests and woodlands; townsites, campgrounds and landfills.

Similar Birds

American Crow

Chihuahuan Raven

shaggy throat

wedge-shaped tail

Nesting: on a ledge, bluff or utility pole or in a tall, coniferous tree; large stick-and-branch nest is lined with fur and soft plant materials; variably marked, greenish eggs are 2 x 1¼ in; female incubates 4–6 eggs for 18–21 days.

Did You Know?

From producing complex vocalizations to playfully sliding down snowbanks, this bird behaves in ways once thought of as exclusively human.

Look For

When working as a pair to procure a meal, one raven may act as the decoy while the other steals the food.

Horned Lark
Eremophila alpestris

An impressive, high-speed, plummeting courtship dive would blow anybody's hair back, or in the case of the Horned Lark, its two unique black "horns." Long before the snow is gone, this bird's tinkling song will be one of the first you hear introducing spring. • Horned Larks are often abundant at roadsides, searching for seeds, but an approaching vehicle usually sends them flying into an adjacent field. When these birds visit in winter, you can spot them in farmers' fields or catch them on lakeshores with Snow Buntings and Lapland Longspurs.

Other ID: *Male:* light yellow to white face; pale throat; dull brown upperparts. *Female:* duller plumage.

Size: *L* 7 in; *W* 12 in.
Voice: call is a tinkling *tsee-titi* or *zoot;* flight song is a long series of tinkling, twittered whistles.
Status: abundant year-round resident at low elevations.

Habitat: open areas, including pastures, native prairie, cultivated or sparsely vegetated fields, golf courses and airfields.

Similar Birds

Snow Bunting

Lapland Longspur

American Pipit

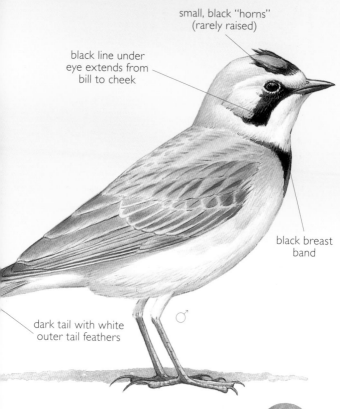

small, black "horns"
(rarely raised)

black line under
eye extends from
bill to cheek

black breast
band

dark tail with white
outer tail feathers

♂

Nesting: on the ground; in a shallow scrape lined with grass, plant fibers and roots; brown-blotched, gray to greenish white eggs are 1 x ⅝ in; female incubates 3–4 eggs for 10–12 days.

Did You Know?

One way to distinguish a sparrow from a Horned Lark is by their method of travel: Horned Larks walk, but sparrows hop.

Look For

This bird's dark tail contrasts with its light brown body and belly. Look for this feature to spot the Horned Lark in its open-country habitat.

Purple Martin
Progne subis

If you set up a luxurious "condo complex" for these large swallows, they will entertain you throughout spring and summer. Martin adults spiral around their accommodations in pursuit of flying insects, while their young perch clumsily at the cavity openings. These birds once nested in natural tree hollows and in cliff crevices, but now they have virtually abandoned these in favor of human-made housing. • To avoid the invasion of aggressive House Sparrows or European Starlings, it is essential for martin condos to be cleaned out and closed up after each nesting season.

Other ID: pointed wings; small bill. *Female:* sooty gray underparts.
Size: L 7–8 in; W 18 in.
Voice: rich, fluty, robinlike *pew-pew*, often heard in flight.
Status: locally common summer resident in western Colorado; common migrant on the eastern plains.
Habitat: semi-open areas, often near water.

Similar Birds

European Starling (p. 178)

Bank Swallow

Northern Rough-winged Swallow

slightly forked tail

♀

glossy, dark blue body

dark underparts

♂

Nesting: communal; in a human-made bird-house or a hollowed-out gourd; nest is made of feathers, grass and mud; white eggs are 1 x ⅝ in; female incubates 4–5 eggs for 15–18 days.

Did You Know?

The Purple Martin is North America's largest swallow.

Look For

These birds are attracted to martin condo complexes erected in open areas, high on a pole and near a body of water.

Cliff Swallow
Petrochelidon pyrrhonota

In recent decades, Cliff Swallows have expanded their range across eastern North America, nesting on various human-made structures, including bridges, culverts and under eaves. During the breeding season, they may be the most abundant swallows in Colorado and are often seen catching insects over agricultural fields and marshes.

• Master mud masons, Cliff Swallows roll mud into balls with their bills and press the pellets together to form their characteristic gourd-shaped nests. Brooding parents peer out of the circular neck of the nest, their gleaming eyes watching the world go by. Their white forehead patch warns intruders that somebody is home.

Other ID: buff breast and rump; whitish belly.
In flight: spotted undertail coverts; nearly square tail.
Size: L 5½ in; W 13½ in.
Voice: twittering chatter, *churrr-churrr*; also an alarm call, *nyew*.
Status: abundant migrant and summer resident with increasing populations.
Habitat: bridges, steep banks, cliffs and buildings; often near watercourses.

Similar Birds

Barn Swallow
(p. 154)

Bank Swallow

Northern Rough-winged Swallow

blue-gray cap

rusty cheek

sharply defined, whitish forehead patch

dark throat

blue-gray wings

Nesting: colonial; under a bridge, on a cliff or under building eaves; pair builds a gourd-shaped mud nest; pale, brown-spotted eggs are ¾ x ⁹⁄₁₆ in; pair incubates 4–5 eggs for 14–16 days.

Did You Know?

A Cliff Swallow will drink on the wing by skimming the water's surface with its open bill.

Look For

This swallow has a square (not forked) tail, a cinnamon-colored rump patch and a distinctive flight pattern, ascending with rapid wing-strokes, then gliding down.

Barn Swallow
Hirundo rustica

When you encounter this bird, you might first notice its distinctive, deeply forked tail—or you might just find yourself repeatedly ducking to avoid the dives of a protective parent. Barn Swallows once nested on cliffs, but they are now more frequently found nesting on barns, boat-houses and areas under bridges and house eaves. • The most widely distributed sparrow in the world, the Barn Swallow breeds over much of North America, Europe, Asia and Africa, and it winters throughout the Southern Hemisphere.

Other ID: blue-black upperparts; long, pointed wings.
Size: *L* 7 in; *W* 15 in.
Voice: continuous, twittering chatter: *zip-zip-zip* or *kvick-kvick*.
Status: abundant migrant and summer resident at lower elevations.
Habitat: open rural and urban areas where bridges, culverts and buildings are found near water.

Similar Birds

Cliff Swallow
(p. 152)

Look For

The deeply forked tail of the Barn Swallow allows it to make tighter turns in flight than other swallows can.

rufous throat
and forehead

black "necklace"

rust- to buff-colored
underparts

long, deeply
forked tail

Nesting: singly or in small, loose colonies; on a human-made structure under an overhang; half or full cup nest is made of mud, grass and straw; brown-spotted, white eggs are ¾ x ½ in; pair incubates 4–7 eggs for 13–17 days.

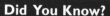

Did You Know?

Because the young are messy and the parents aggressive, people unfortunately sometimes remove nests just as the nesting season is beginning. However, the Barn Swallow is a natural pest controller, feeding on insects that are often troublesome or harmful to crops and livestock.

Mountain Chickadee
Poecile gambeli

This year-round resident of high-elevation forests spends much of its time feeding on seeds and insects high in a canopy of conifers. During winter, harsh weather can cause Mountain Chickadees to freeze or starve, and many birds move to lower elevations in search of warmer temperatures and more abundant food. • The Mountain Chickadee breeds at higher elevations than most other chickadees. It routinely nests in subalpine conifers between 6000 and 8500 feet and is often seen foraging up to the treeline.

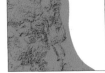

Other ID: light gray upperparts and tail; light gray or tan underparts.
Size: *L* 5¼ in; *W* 8½ in.
Voice: song is sweet, clear, whistled *fee-bee-bay* or *fee-bay*; call is drawling *chick a-day, day, day*.
Status: fairly common year-round resident in the foothills and mountains.
Habitat: montane coniferous forests and lower portions of subalpine forests; irregular downslope flights to lowlands and foothills.

Similar Birds

Black-capped Chickadee

White-breasted
Nuthatch (p. 158)

white eyebrow through black cap

white cheek

black "bib"

drab, gray wings

Nesting: in a natural cavity or abandoned woodpecker nest; can excavate a cavity in soft, rotting wood; lines the nest with fur, feathers, moss and grass; usually unspotted, white eggs are ⅝ x ½ in; incubates 5–9 eggs for up to 14 days.

Did You Know?

The scientific descriptor *gambeli* honors William Gambel, a 19th-century ornithologist who died of typhoid fever in the Sierra Nevada at the age of 28.

Look For

During winter, feeders in mountain townsites, where Black-capped and Mountain chickadees often forage together, offer excellent viewing opportunities.

White-breasted Nuthatch

Sitta carolinensis

Whether you spot this small, black-capped bird spiraling headfirst down a tree or clinging to the underside of a branch in search of invertebrates, the nuthatch's odd behavior deserves a second glance.
• Comparing the White-breasted Nuthatch to the Black-capped Chickadee, both regular visitors to backyard feeders, is a perfect starting point for introductory birding. These similar-sized cavity nesters both have dark crowns and gray backs, but the nuthatch's foraging behaviors and undulating flight pattern are distinct.

Other ID: white underparts; white face; straight bill; short legs. *Female:* dark gray cap.
Size: L 5½–6 in; W 11 in.
Voice: song is a fast, nasal *yank-hank yank-hank,* lower than the Red-breasted Nuthatch; calls include *ha-ha-ha ha-ha-ha, ank ank* and *ip.*
Status: fairly common year-round resident in the foothills and lower mountains.
Habitat: mixed forests, woodlots and backyards.

Similar Birds

Red-breasted Nuthatch

Black-capped Chickadee

Mountain Chickadee (p. 156)

rusty undertail coverts

short tail

gray-blue back

dark crown

♀

♂

Nesting: in a natural cavity or an abandoned woodpecker nest; female lines the cavity with soft material; white eggs, speckled with brown are ¾ x ⁹⁄₁₆ in; female incubates 5–8 eggs for 12–14 days.

Did You Know?

Nuthatches are presumably named for their habit of wedging seeds and nuts into crevices and hacking them open with their bills.

Look For

Nuthatches grasp the tree through foot power alone, unlike woodpeckers, which use their tails to brace themselves against tree trunks.

Rock Wren
Salpinctes obsoletus

Well-camouflaged plumage, secretive habits and echoing songs and calls can make the Rock Wren difficult to spot. Singing males are experts at remaining concealed while bouncing their buzzy, trilling songs off canyon walls, maximizing the range and aural effect of the sound. • Rock Wren nests may be built in a sheltered, rocky crevice, in an animal burrow or even in an abandoned building. Nest entrances are typically "paved" with a few small pebbles, bones or other debris. Occasionally the entrances contain up to 1600 small items!

Other ID: large wren; short, white eyebrow; buffy underparts. *In flight:* cinnamon rump.
Size: L 6 in; W 9 in.
Voice: repeated, accented 1–2-note phrases: *tra-lee tra-lee tra-lee*; alarm call is *tick-EAR*.
Status: fairly common summer resident in the foothills and lower mountains; fairly common on the plains during migration.
Habitat: talus slopes, scree, outcrops, stony barrens or similar substrate with abundant crevices.

Similar Birds

Canyon Wren

House Wren (p. 162)

Bewick's Wren

slender bill

blue-gray to gray-brown upperparts with intricate light and dark flecking

finely streaked, white throat and breast

tail is trimmed with buff-colored tips

Nesting: in a crevice, hole or burrow; often places small stones at the opening; nest of grass and rootlets is lined with a variety of items; white, speckled eggs are ¾ x ⁹⁄₁₆ in; female incubates 5–6 eggs for up to 14 days.

Did You Know?

Salpinctes is Greek for "trumpeter," referring to this bird's exclamatory call, and *obsoletus* is Latin for "indistinct," referring to the bird's dull, cryptic plumage.

Look For

Rock Wrens are typically identified at long range by their habit of bobbing atop prominent boulders.

House Wren
Troglodytes aedon

The nondescript plumage of this suburban and city park dweller can be overlooked until you hear the wren sing a seemingly unending song in one breath. The voice of the House Wren is as sweet as that of a nightingale. Despite the light-hearted, bubbly nature of its tune, this wren can be very aggressive toward other species that nest in its territory, puncturing and tossing eggs from other bird's nests. A House Wren often builds numerous nests, which later serve as decoys or "dummy" nests to fool would-be predators.

Other ID: brown upperparts; whitish throat; faintly barred flanks; whitish to buff underparts.
Size: L 4½–5 in; W 6 in.
Voice: smooth, running, bubbly warble: *tsi-tsi-tsi-tsi oodle-oodle-oodle-oodle.*
Status: common summer resident in valleys, foothills and the lower mountains.
Habitat: thickets and shrubby openings in or at the edge of deciduous or mixed woodlands; often in shrubs and thickets near buildings.

Similar Birds

Winter Wren

Red-breasted
Nuthatch

short, upraised tail is finely barred with black

fine, dark barring on upperwings and lower back

faint, pale eyebrow and eye ring

Nesting: in a natural or artificial cavity or an abandoned woodpecker nest; nest of sticks and grass is lined with feathers and fur; heavily marked, white eggs are ⅝ x ½ in; female incubates 6–8 eggs for 12–15 days.

Did You Know?

This bird has the largest range of any New World passerine, stretching from Canada to southern South America.

Look For

Like all wrens, the House Wren usually carries its short tail raised upward.

American Dipper
Cinclus mexicanus

When you come across a small, dark bird standing on an exposed boulder next to a fast-flowing mountain stream, you have no doubt found an American Dipper. This unique aquatic songbird bends its legs incessantly, bobbing to the roar of the torrent, then suddenly dives into the water in search of aquatic insects. Fitted with scaly nose plugs, strong claws, dense plumage, inner eyelids to protect against water spray and an oil gland to waterproof its feathers, the American Dipper survives a lifetime of these ice-cold forays.

Other ID: whitish eyelid visible when bird blinks; pinkish legs; straight, black bill; stout body. *Immature:* paler bill; paler underparts.
Size: *L* 7½ in; *W* 11 in (male slightly larger than female).
Voice: vocal throughout the year; warbled song is clear and melodious; alarm call is harsh *tzeet*.
Status: uncommon year-round resident in the foothills and mountains.
Habitat: *Breeding:* swift, clear, cold, permanent mountain streams with boulders and often waterfalls; subalpine tarns. *Winter:* also in larger, slower-flowing rivers and lowland lakes.

Look For

These birds use their wings to "fly" under water, making their way along the streambed in search of hidden aquatic insect larvae. They walk easily in shallow water, using their long toes to grasp the gravelly bottom.

short tail

head and neck
darker than body

slate gray plumage

Nesting: built into a rock ledge, overhang,
uprooted tree or under a bridge; female builds
bulky globe nest of moss and grass; nest
entrance faces water; white eggs are 1 x ¾ in;
female incubates 4–5 eggs for up to 17 days.

Did You Know?

The dipper's well-constructed nest may be used year after
year and is always built near water. The nest may even be
placed on a cliff behind a waterfall, in which case the dipper
will fly right through the rushing water on journeys to and
from its nest.

Ruby-crowned Kinglet

Regulus calendula

This kinglet's familiar voice echoes through our boreal forest in spring and summer. Not only does the male Ruby-crowned Kinglet possess a loud, complex, warbling song to bring him some attention, but he also wears a nifty red "mohawk" to help attract a mate and defend his territory in spring. Unfortunately, his distinctive crown is only visible in the breeding season, leaving him with just his dull olive green plumage for the rest of the year.

Other ID: dark wings; olive green upperparts; whitish to yellowish underparts; flicks its wings.
Size: *L* 4 in; *W* 7½ in.
Voice: *Male:* song is an accelerating and rising *tea-tea-tea-tew-tew-tew* look-at-Me, look-at-Me, look-at-Me.
Status: common summer resident in the higher mountains; fairly common migrant west of the plains.
Habitat: mixed woodlands and pure coniferous forests, especially with spruce; often near wet forest openings and edges.

Similar Birds

Golden-crowned Kinglet

Orange-crowned Warbler

bold, broken eye ring

♀

small, red crown is usually hidden

short, dark tail

2 white wing bars

♂

Nesting: usually in a conifer; female builds a hanging nest of lichen, twigs and leaves; brown-spotted, white to pale buff eggs are ½ x ⅜ in; female incubates 7–8 eggs for 13–14 days.

Did You Know?

Females can lay an impressively large clutch with up to 12 eggs, which together often weigh as much as the bird that laid them!

Look For

Watch for this bird's hovering technique and wing-flicking behavior to distinguish it from similar-looking flycatchers.

Mountain Bluebird
Sialia currucoides

The vibrant Mountain Bluebird looks like a piece of sky come to life. It perches on wire fences and tall grasses, alighting to snatch up insects on the ground or hovering briefly to pluck at berries.
• Natural nest sites, such as woodpecker cavities or holes in sandstone cliffs, are in high demand. Habitat loss and increased competition with aggressive European Starlings for these sites have forced many mild-mannered bluebirds to nest in artificial nest boxes.

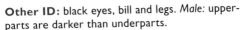

Other ID: black eyes, bill and legs. *Male:* upperparts are darker than underparts.
Size: *L* 7 in; *W* 14 in.
Voice: call is a low *turr turr;* male's song is a short warble of *chur* notes.
Status: common migrant and summer resident west of the plains; some birds winter in lower elevations of southwestern Colorado.
Habitat: open forests, forest edges, burned forests, agricultural areas and grasslands.

Similar Birds

Western Bluebird

Eastern Bluebird

Townsend's Solitaire

brownish gray overall

sky blue wings, tail and rump

♀

♂

sky blue body

white undertail coverts

Nesting: in an abandoned woodpecker cavity, natural cavity or nest box; cavity is lined with plant stems, grass, conifer needles, twigs and feathers; pale blue eggs are ⅞ x ⅝ in; female incubates 5–6 eggs for 13 days.

Did You Know?

Mountain Bluebirds often raise two broods per year, and fledglings may help gather food for the second clutch.

Look For

Recently burned areas attract bluebirds, which nest in abandoned woodpecker cavities found in the snags.

Hermit Thrush

Catharus guttatus

The Hermit Thrush's haunting, flutelike song may be one of the most beautiful natural melodies. The clear song is a familiar theme on nesting grounds, as much a part of the forest ecosystem as are the trees and wildflowers. The song of the Hermit Thrush is almost always preceded with a single questioning note—a trait shared by the Swainson's Thrush • For the first two days after arriving in a male's territory, a female Hermit Thrush will be attacked and chased. If the female still remains after these two days, the male gradually accepts her and the union is formed.

Other ID: thin bill; pale underparts; gray flanks; pink legs.
Size: *L* 7 in; *W* 11½ in.
Voice: song is a series of beautiful flutelike notes, both rising and falling in pitch; a small questioning note may precede the song; calls include a faint *chuck* and a fluty *treee*.
Status: fairly common summer resident in the foothills and mountains, especially at higher elevations; fairly common migrant on the eastern plains and western plateaus.
Habitat: deciduous, mixed or coniferous woodlands; wet coniferous bogs bordered by trees.

Similar Birds

Swainson's Thrush

Veery

Gray-cheeked Thrush

reddish brown tail and rump

grayish brown upperparts

thin, whitish eye ring

black-spotted throat and breast

Nesting: usually on or near the ground; female builds a bulky cup nest of vegetation; blue to greenish blue eggs, sometimes with dark flecks, are ⅞ x ⅝ in; female incubates 4 pale eggs for 11–13 days.

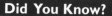

Did You Know?

The scientific name *guttatus* is Latin for "spotted" or "speckled," in reference to this bird's breast.

Look For

Unlike similar thrushes, the Hermit Thrush flicks its wings and tail while perched.

American Robin
Turdus migratorius

In spring, the familiar song of the American Robin may wake you early if you are a light sleeper. This abundant bird adapts easily to urban areas and often works from dawn until after dusk when there is a nest to be built or hungry, young mouths to feed. • The robin's bright red belly contrasts with its dark head and wings, making this bird easy to identify. • In winter, fruit trees may attract flocks of robins, which gather to drink the fermenting fruit's intoxicating juices.

Other ID: incomplete, white eye ring; gray-brown back; white under-tail coverts.
Size: L 10 in; W 17 in.
Voice: song is an evenly spaced warble: *cheerily cheer-up cheerio;* call is a rapid *tut-tut-tut.*
Status: common resident statewide, except in winter when common only locally.
Habitat: *Breeding:* residential lawns and gardens, pastures, urban parks, broken forests, bogs and river shorelines. *Winter:* near fruit-bearing trees and springs.

Similar Birds

Varied Thrush

Look For

A hunting robin with its head tilted to the side isn't listening for prey—it is actually looking for movements in the soil.

black head

dark gray head

black-tipped, yellow bill

white throat is streaked with black

♂ ♀

brick red breast is darker on male

Nesting: in a tree or shrub; cup nest is built of grass, moss, bark and mud; light blue eggs are 1⅛ x ¾ in; female incubates 4 eggs for 11–16 days; raises up to 3 broods per year.

Did You Know?

American Robins do not use nest boxes; they prefer plat-forms for their nests. Robins usually raise two broods per year, with the male caring for the fledglings from the first brood while the female incubates the second clutch of eggs.

Northern Mockingbird

Mimus polyglottos

Northern Mockingbirds are great entertainers with a lot to say. Their amazing vocal repertoire includes over 400 different song types that they belt out incessantly during the breeding season. Mockingbirds can imitate almost anything, from the vocalizations of other birds and animals to musical instruments. In fact, they replicate notes so accurately that even computerized sound analysis has been unable to detect the difference between the original source and the mockingbird's imitation.

Other ID: gray upperparts; 2 thin, white wing bars.
In flight: large, white patch at base of black primaries.
Size: *L* 10 in; *W* 14 in.
Voice: song is a medley of mimicked phrases that are often repeated 3 times or more; calls include a harsh *chair* and *chewk*.
Status: fairly common migrant and summer resident in the southeast; uncommon elsewhere.
Habitat: hedges, suburban gardens and orchard margins with abundant fruit; hedgerows of multiflora roses, especially in winter.

Similar Birds

Loggerhead Shrike
(p. 134)

Townsend's Solitaire

Gray Catbird

long, dark tail with white
outer tail feathers

thin, dark eye line

dark wings

light gray
underparts

Nesting: often in a small shrub or small tree; cup nest is built with twigs and plants; brown-blotched, bluish gray to greenish eggs are 1 x ⅝ in; female incubates 3–4 eggs for 12–13 days.

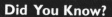

Did You Know?

The scientific name *poly-glottos* is Greek for "many tongues" and refers to this bird's ability to mimic a wide variety of sounds.

Look For

In winter, generous offerings of suet, raisins and fruit at feeders can lure these and other birds into your yard.

Sage Thrasher
Oreoscoptes montanus

The Sage Thrasher, the smallest of our thrashers, is intricately linked to the open flats of sagebrush of the western United States. These thrashers are regularly seen perched on the tops of sage and other shrubs, belting out long, warbling phrases. • Though drab in color, the Sage Thrasher has a harmonious, flutelike song that may be heard throughout the day  during the breeding season and into the night during a full moon. This bird is also an accomplished mimic of other species, especially the Western Meadowlark and the Horned Lark. It was originally named the "Sagebrush Mockingbird."

Other ID: gray-brown upperparts. *In flight:* white tail corners.
Size: *L* 8½ in; *W* 12 in.
Voice: the male's long, complex, warbled song includes repeated phrases; high *churr* and *chuck* calls; a notable night singer.
Status: fairly common throughout Colorado during migration; common summer resident in the northwest.
Habitat: sagebrush shrublands; open brushland dominated by tall sagebrush.

Similar Birds

Northern
Mockingbird (p. 174)

Brown Thrasher

Curve-billed Thrasher

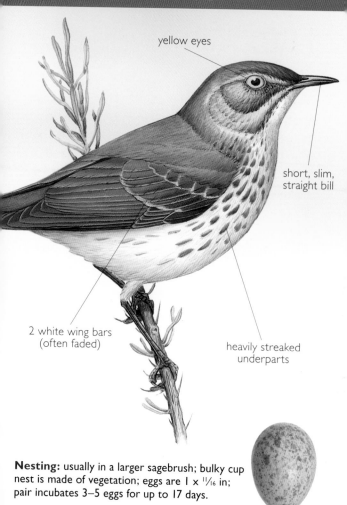

yellow eyes

short, slim, straight bill

2 white wing bars (often faded)

heavily streaked underparts

Nesting: usually in a larger sagebrush; bulky cup nest is made of vegetation; eggs are 1 x ¹¹⁄₁₆ in; pair incubates 3–5 eggs for up to 17 days.

Did You Know?

"Thrasher" is derived from "thrush"—thrashers belong to the family Mimidae, the mimic thrushes.

Look For

While perched, the Sage Thrasher slowly raises and lowers its tail, and when running along the ground, it holds its tail high, much like a mockingbird.

European Starling
Sturnus vulgaris

The European Starling did not hesitate to make itself known across North America after being released in New York's Central Park in 1890 and 1891. This highly adaptable bird not only took over the nest sites of native cavity nesters, such as Tree Swallows and Red-headed Woodpeckers, but it also learned to mimic the sounds of Killdeers, Red-tailed Hawks, Soras and meadowlarks. • Look for European Starlings in massive evening roosts under bridges or on buildings.

Other ID: dark eyes; short, squared tail.
Nonbreeding: feather tips are heavily spotted with white and buff.
Size: L 8½ in; W 16 in.
Voice: variety of whistles, squeaks and gurgles; imitates other birds.
Status: abundant year-round resident at lower elevations; fairly common else-where except at the highest elevations.
Habitat: *Breeding:* cities, towns, resi-dential areas, farmyards, woodland fringes and clearings. *Winter:* near feed-lots and pastures.

Similar Birds

Rusty Blackbird

Brewer's Blackbird

Brown-headed Cowbird (p. 218)

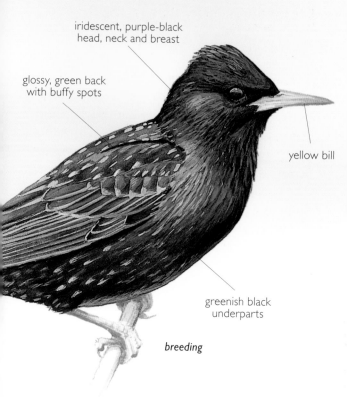

iridescent, purple-black
head, neck and breast

glossy, green back
with buffy spots

yellow bill

greenish black
underparts

breeding

Nesting: in an abandoned woodpecker cavity,
natural cavity or nest box; nest is made of
grass, twigs and straw; bluish to greenish white
eggs are 1⅛ x ⅞ in; female incubates 4–6 eggs
for 12–14 days.

Did You Know?

Starlings were brought to
New York as part of the
local Shakespeare society's
plan to introduce all the
birds mentioned in their
favorite author's writings.

Look For

The European Starling can be
confused for a blackbird, but
note the starling's shorter tail
and bright yellow bill.

Cedar Waxwing
Bombycilla cedrorum

With its black mask and slick hairdo, the Cedar Waxwing has a heroic look. This bird's splendid personality is reflected in its amusing antics after it gorges on fermented berries and in its gentle courtship ritual. To court a mate, the gentlemanly male hops toward a female and offers her a berry. The female accepts the berry and hops away, then stops and hops back toward the male to offer him the berry in return. • If a bird's crop is full and it is unable to eat any more, it will continue to pluck fruit and pass it down the line, like a bucket brigade, until the fruit is gulped down by a still-hungry bird.

Other ID: brown upperparts; yellow wash on belly; gray rump; white undertail coverts.

Size: *L* 7 in; *W* 12 in.

Voice: faint, high-pitched, trilled whistle: *tseee-tseee-tseee*.

Status: locally uncommon during summer; nomadic and unpredictable breeder; irregular visitor in small flocks to river valleys, foothills and lower mountains in winter.

Habitat: wooded residential parks and gardens, overgrown fields, forest edges; second-growth, riparian and open woodlands; often near fruit trees and water.

Similar Birds

Bohemian Waxwing

Look For

Waxwings will show definite signs of tipsiness after consuming fermented fruit.

cinnamon crest

black mask

small red "drops" on wings

yellow wash on belly

yellow terminal tail band

Nesting: in a tree or shrub; cup nest is made of twigs, moss and lichen; darkly spotted, bluish to gray eggs are ⅞ x ⅝ in; female incubates 3–5 eggs for 12–16 days.

Did You Know?

The Cedar Waxwing is one of the latest-nesting birds in North America. Because it's primary food source is fruit, egg hatching must coincide with the ripening of summer fruits in late spring and summer.

Yellow Warbler

Dendroica petechia

The nest of the Yellow Warbler is often parasitized by the Brown-headed Cowbird. This warbler can recognize the cowbird eggs, but rather than tossing them out, it will build another nest overtop the old eggs or abandon the nest site completely. Occasionally, cowbirds strike repeatedly—a five-story nest was once found! • The widely distributed Yellow Warbler arrives in May, flitting from branch to branch in search of juicy caterpillars, aphids and beetles and singing its *sweet-sweet* song. • It is often mistakenly called "Wild Canary."

Other ID: bright yellow body; yellowish legs; black bill and eyes. *Female:* may have faint, red breast streaks.
Size: L 5 in; W 8 in.
Voice: song is a fast, frequently repeated *sweet-sweet-sweet summer sweet*.
Status: fairly common migrant and summer resident, except at the highest elevations.
Habitat: habitat generalist; moist, open woodlands, dense scrub, scrubby meadows, second-growth woodlands, riparian woods and urban parks and gardens.

Similar Birds

Orange-crowned
Warbler

American Goldfinch
(p. 226)

Wilson's Warbler
(p. 186)

♀

♂

red breast streaks

bright yellow
highlights on dark
olive yellow tail
and wings

Nesting: in a deciduous tree or shrub; female builds a cup nest of grass, weeds and shredded bark; darkly speckled, greenish white eggs are ⅝ x ½ in; female incubates eggs for 11–12 days.

Did You Know?

The Yellow Warbler has an amazing geographical range. It is found throughout North America and on islands in Central and South America.

Look For

In fall, when male Yellow Warblers are no longer in breeding plumage, look for flashes of yellow on the sides of their tails to identify them.

Yellow-rumped Warbler

Dendroica coronata

Yellow-rumped Warblers are the most abundant and widespread wood-warblers in North America. • This species comes in two forms: the common, yellow-throated "Audubon's Warbler" of the West, and the white-throated "Myrtle Warbler," breeding in Canada and the northeastern U.S. Although "Myrtles" do not breed our state, they are commonly on the eastern plains during migration.

Other ID: *"Myrtle Warbler":* white chin; thin, white eye line; strong streaking beneath black cheek and breast band; two white wing bars. *Breeding female (both subspecies):* gray-brown upperparts; fainter yellow patches; faint brown breast streaks.
Size: L 5½ in; W 9¼ in.
Voice: song is a brief, bubbling warble rising or falling at the end, with much variation between races and individuals; call is a sharp *chip* or *chet.*
Status: common migrant on the eastern plains; uncommon breeder in the western valleys.
Habitat: a variety of well-vegetated habitats in lowlands, especially in wax myrtle thickets.

Similar Birds

Townsend's Warbler

Black-throated Green Warbler

Cape May Warbler

yellow shoulder patch

yellow crown

blue-gray upperparts with black streaking

bright yellow rump

♀

♂

blackish breast and sides

"Audubon Warbler"
breeding

Nesting: in a crotch or on a horizontal limb in a conifer; female constructs a compact cup nest with grass, bark strips, moss, lichens and spider silk; pale buff, blotched eggs are ⅝ x ½ in; female incubates 4–5 eggs for up to 13 days.

Did You Know?

This small warbler's habit of flitting near buildings to snatch spiders from their webs has earned it the nickname "Spider Bird."

Look For

Small puddles that form during or after rains often attract warblers, allowing a glimpse of these secretive birds.

Wilson's Warbler

Wilsonia pusilla

One of Colorado's more common warbler migrants, the petite Wilson's Warbler darts energetically through the undergrowth in its tireless search for insects. Fueled by its energy-rich prey, this untiring bird seems to behave as if a motionless moment would break some unwritten law of warblerdom. • Breeding occurs solely in higher-elevation riparian thickets of western Colorado, so birders on the plains are forced to go without this beauty during the breeding season. Shrubs still laden with heavy spring snow often greet Wilson's Warblers arriving in their subalpine breeding grounds at the beginning of May.

Other ID: large, beady eyes; thin, black bill.
Female: cap is faint, partial or absent.
Size: L 4½–5 in; W 7 in.
Voice: song is loud, staccato chatter that accelerates toward the end: *chi chi chi chi chi chi chet chet;* call is soft, brittle *chet.*
Status: common statewide migrant; common summer resident in the higher mountains.
Habitat: shrubby, riparian habitat; also uses wet mountain meadows and edges of small lakes and springs.

Similar Birds

Yellow Warbler
(p. 182)

Common
Yellowthroat

Orange-crowned
Warbler

yellowish green
upperparts

black cap

♀

♂

frail-looking,
orange legs

yellow underparts

Nesting: sunken into soft ground or in a low shrub; female builds a neat cup nest of vegetation; brown-spotted, whitish eggs are ⅝ x ½ in; female incubates 4–6 eggs for 10–13 days.

Did You Know?

This bird is named for ornithologist Alexander Wilson, who pioneered studies of North American birds.

Look For

During the breeding season, energetic Wilson's Warblers are often found in cool, moist riparian habitat with dense deciduous shrub cover, especially willow and alder.

Yellow-breasted Chat
Icteria virens

At a length of nearly 8 inches, the Yellow-breasted Chat is quite literally a "warbler and a half." This bird is an official member of the wood-warbler clan: its bright yellow coloration and intense curiosity are typical traits of the warblers. However, the chat's large size, curious vocalizations and noisy thrashing behavior suggest a closer relationship to the mimic thrushes, such as the Gray Catbird and Northern Mockingbird. • Often heard but difficult to see, this elusive bird avoids detection by skulking through brushy riparian thickets and tangled fencerows.

Other ID: white jaw line; heavy, black bill; olive green upperparts; gray-black legs. *Female:* gray lores.
Size: L 7½ in; W 9¾ in.
Voice: single notes or phrases of slurred piping whistles, *kuks*, harsh rattles and "laughs"; persistent night singing in spring.
Status: fairly common summer resident in the foothills and mesas.
Habitat: dense riparian thickets bordering streams; small ponds and swampy ground dominated by vine tangles; willows and lush, low shrubbery interspersed by taller trees such as alder and cottonwood; may breed in extensive hillside bramble-patches.

Look For

During courtship, the male advertises for a mate by launching off his perch, hovering with his head held high and legs dangling, and chirping incessantly. Males and females arrive separately on their breeding grounds, pairing up only once they arrive, unlike some species that pair up on wintering grounds or during migration.

white "spectacles"

black lores

♂

yellow breast

white undertail coverts

Nesting: low in a shrub or a small tree; well-concealed, bulky nest is made of leaves, straw and weeds, with a tight inner cup woven with bark and plant fibers; white eggs with variable markings are ⅞ x ⅝ in; female incubates 3–4 eggs for about 11 days.

Did You Know?

Yellow-breasted Chats are well known for singing at night during spring. Only the males sing, and they have a repertoire of highly variable songs. A male chat may sing, on average, 60 different songs, which may include phrases mimicked from other bird species.

Western Tanager

Piranga ludoviciana

Western Tanagers bring with them the colors of the tropics on their short stay in our state. They raise a new generation of young and take advantage of the seasonal explosion of food in our forests before heading back to their exotic wintering grounds in Mexico and Central America. • Despite the male's stunning plumage, accentuated by black wings and a black tail, the Western Tanager might take some patience to spot. The male's song can also be a challenge to recognize. It closely parallels the robin's tune, but the Western Tanager sings it with what sounds like a sore throat.

Other ID: *Breeding male:* black back, wings and tail; often has red on forehead or entire head. *Breeding female:* lighter underparts; darker upperparts.
Size: *L* 7 in; *W* 11–11½ in.
Voice: call is a hiccupy *pit-a-tik*. *Male:* song is hoarse and robinlike: *hurry, scurry, scurry, hurry.*
Status: fairly common migrant and summer resident in the foothills and lower mountains.
Habitat: mature coniferous forests, especially Douglas-fir or mixedwood forests and trembling aspen or poplar woodlands.

Similar Birds

Baltimore Oriole

Bullock's Oriole
(p. 220)

faint wing bars

olive green overall

pale bill

♀

♂

breeding

yellow underparts, wing bars and rump

Nesting: on a horizontal branch or fork in a conifer, well out from the trunk; cup nest is loosely built of twigs, grass and other plant materials and lined with finer vegetation; brown-spotted, light blue or greenish eggs are ⅞ x ⅝ in; female incubates 4 eggs for 13–14 days.

Did You Know?

"Tanager" is derived from *tangara,* the Tupi Indian name for this group of birds in the Amazon Basin of South America.

Look For

The male Western Tanager spends long periods of time singing from the same perch.

Green-tailed Towhee
Pipilo chlorurus

Green-tailed Towhees are birds of arid scrub habitats in the western foothills and lower mountains. They can be common summer birds of hillsides and foothills, while remaining entirely unknown in the nearby valleys. These birds spend most of their lives concealed in shrubby undergrowth, industriously scratching away debris with both feet in their search for insects and hidden seeds. If a threat is presented, they will unwillingly flush or run from cover, giving an annoyed "mewing" call.

Other ID: sooty gray face; gray legs; conical, gray bill. *Immature:* brownish overall; streaked upperparts and underparts; pale throat bordered by dark stripe and white stripe.

Size: L 6½–7 in; W 9¾ in.

Voice: song is a series of clear, whistled notes followed by squealing, raspy trills: *swee-too weet chur cheee-churr;* call is a distinctive, nasal *mew.*

Status: common migrant and summer resident in the foothills and lower mountains.

Habitat: arid, shrubby hillsides featuring sagebrush, juniper or other well-spaced trees and shrubs; also found in dense, low thickets.

Similar Birds

Fox Sparrow

Rufous-crowned Sparrow

rufous orange crown

yellowish green upper-parts, most intense on wings and tail

white throat with dark stripe

gray breast

Nesting: on or near the ground; deep, bulky cup nest of twigs, grass and bark shreds is lined with fine materials; darkly spotted, white eggs are ⅞ x ⅝ in; female incubates 3–4 eggs for 11 days.

Did You Know?

Pipilo is derived from a Latin word meaning "to twitter"; *chlorurus* means "green tail."

Look For

The best time to see a Green-tailed Towhee is in spring, when the male gives clear, whistled notes, raspy trills or catlike *mew* calls from an exposed woody perch.

Spotted Towhee
Pipilo maculatus

Don't be disappointed if the raccoon you were expecting to see at close range turns out to be a bird not much larger than a sparrow. The Spotted Towhee is capable of quite a ruckus when it forages in loose leaf litter, scraping with both feet.

• Although a confident bird, not hesitant to scold even the family cat, the Spotted Towhee can be shy. It needs some coaxing if you want to lure it into the open, and it tends to make itself scarce in a park crowded with people.

Other ID: white spotting on wings and back; white outer tail corners; white breast and belly; buffy undertail. *Female:* paler overall.
Size: L 7–8 in; W 10–10½ in.
Voice: song is *here here here PLEASE*; distinctive call is a buzzy trill.
Status: fairly common summer resident in the foothills and mesas; migrates to the southern foothills in winter.
Habitat: brushy hedgerows and woods with a dense understory; overgrown bushy fields and hillsides; frequently at feeders, especially in winter.

Similar Birds

Dark-eyed "Oregon" Junco (p. 204)

Look For

The Spotted Towhee especially likes tangled thickets and overgrown gardens with blackberries and other small fruits.

black hood, back, wings and tail

red eyes

dark, conical bill

♂

dark rufous sides and flanks

Nesting: low in a shrub or in a depression on the ground; cup of leaves, bark and rootlets is lined with fine grass and hair; brown-wreathed, white eggs are 1 x ¾ in; pair incubates 3–4 eggs for 12–13 days.

Did You Know?

Until recently, the Spotted Towhee was grouped together with the Eastern Towhee as a single species called the "Rufous-sided Towhee." The Spotted Towhee is more commonly found in the western part of North America.

Chipping Sparrow

Spizella passerina

Though you may spot the relatively tame Chipping Sparrow singing from a high perch, it commonly nests at eye level, so you can easily watch its breeding and nest-building rituals. You can even take part in the building of this bird's nest by leaving samples of your pet's hair—or your own—around your backyard. • This bird's song is very similar to that of the Dark-eyed Junco. Listen for a slightly faster, drier and less musical series of notes to identify the Chipping Sparrow.

Other ID: *Breeding:* mottled brown upperparts; light gray, unstreaked underparts; dark bill. *Nonbreeding:* paler crown with dark streaks; brown eyebrow and cheek; pale lower mandible.
Size: *L* 5–6 in; *W* 8½ in.
Voice: song is a rapid, dry trill of *chip* notes; call is a high-pitched *chip*.
Status: fairly common statewide in migration; common summer resident in the west.
Habitat: open conifers or mixed woodland edges; yards and gardens with tree and shrub borders.

Similar Birds

American Tree Sparrow

Field Sparrow

prominent rufous cap

white eyebrow

black eye line

white wing bars

breeding

Nesting: usually at mid-level in a coniferous tree; female builds a cup nest of grass and rootlets lined with hair; pale blue eggs are ¾ x ½ in; female incubates 4 eggs for 11–12 days.

Did You Know?

The Chipping Sparrow is the most common and widely distributed migrating sparrow in North America.

Look For

Chipping Sparrows visit feeders and forage on lawns for the seeds of grasses, dandelions and clovers.

Lark Bunting
Calamospiza melanocorys

Unlike most sparrows, the male Lark Bunting trades in his cryptic winter plumage for bold black and white breeding colors. In spring, he performs a spectacular courtship flight over grasslands and hay fields. As he rises into the air, he flutters about in circles above the plains, beating his wings slowly and deeply. His bell-like, tinkling song spreads over the landscape until he folds his wings and floats to the ground like a falling leaf. • The Lark Bunting is Colorado's state bird.

Other ID: *Female:* mottled brown upperparts; very bold, lateral throat stripe; heavily streaked underparts; pale eyebrow; obvious white-edged inner wing in flight. *Nonbreeding male:* similar to female but with darker streaking.
Size: *L* 7 in; *W* 10½ in.
Voice: rich and warbling, with clear notes.
Status: abundant migrant and summer resident on the eastern plains and in northwestern Colorado.
Habitat: short-grass and mixed-grass prairie, sagebrush, hay fields, grassy ditches and lightly grazed pastures.

Similar Birds

Savannah Sparrow   Lark Sparrow   Bobolink

dark, conical bill

bright white
wing patch

black plumage

♂   *breeding*

white patch at
tip of tail

Nesting: on the ground, sheltered by grass or a small bush; loose cup nest of plant material is lined with plant down and fur; pale blue eggs are ⅞ x ⅝ in; mostly female incubates 4–5 eggs for 11–12 days.

Did You Know?

This bird is actually a sparrow and is one of only six songbirds that are found only in the North American grasslands.

Look For

In certain areas, the Lark Bunting is a common sight along roads because it breeds in roadside ditches, hay fields and native short- and mixed-grass prairies.

Song Sparrow
Melospiza melodia

Although its plumage is unremarkable, the well-named Song Sparrow is among the great singers of the bird world. By the time a young male Song Sparrow is only a few months old, he has already created a courtship tune of his own, having learned the basics of melody and rhythm from his father and rival males. • In winter, adaptable Song Sparrows are common throughout Colorado, in woodland edges, weedy ditches and riparian thickets. They regularly visit backyard feeders, belting out their sweet, three-part song throughout the year.

Other ID: white jaw line; mottled brown upper-parts; rounded tail tip.
Size: L 6–7 in; W 8 in.
Voice: song is 1–4 introductory notes, such as *sweet sweet sweet,* followed by a buzzy *towee,* then a short, descending trill; call is short *tsip* or *tchep.*
Status: fairly common year-round resident, except at the highest elevations.
Habitat: willow shrublands, riparian thickets, forest openings and pastures, all usually near water.

Similar Birds

Swamp Sparrow

Fox Sparrow

Lincoln's Sparrow

brown line behind eye

dark crown with pale central stripe

grayish face

dark "mustache" stripe

heavy brown streaks converge at central breast spot

Nesting: usually on the ground or in a low shrub; female builds an open cup nest of grass, weeds and bark strips; brown-blotched, greenish white eggs are ⅞ x ⅝ in; female incubates 3–5 eggs for 12–14 days.

Did You Know?

Though female songbirds are not usually vocal, the female Song Sparrow will occasionally sing a tune of her own.

Look For

The Song Sparrow pumps its long, rounded tail in flight. It also often issues a high-pitched *seet* flight call.

White-crowned Sparrow

Zonotrichia leucophrys

Large, bold and smartly patterned, White-crowned Sparrows brighten many high-elevation brushy expanses and wet meadows in summer with varied songs. At least three different races of the White-crowned Sparrow occur in Colorado, so not all birds sound alike, but they all give a slight variation of *I-I-I-got-to-go-wee-wee-now!*

Other ID: streaked brown back. *Immature:* head stripes are brown and gray, not black and white.
Size: *L* 5½–7 in; *W* 9½ in.
Voice: frequent *I-I-I-got-to-go-wee-wee-now!;* call is a hard *pink* or high *seep.*
Status: common migrant at lower elevations; common summer resident at higher elevations; common winter resident on the eastern plains.
Habitat: *Breeding:* wet, shrubby meadows, stunted montane forest, thickets. *In migration* and *winter:* woodlots, parkland edges, brushy tangles, riparian thickets; also open, weedy fields, lawns and roadsides.

Similar Birds

White-throated Sparrow

Golden-crowned Sparrow

orange-pink bill

bold, black and white head stripes

gray face

2 white wing bars

gray, unstreaked underparts

Nesting: in a shrub, small conifer or on the ground; neat cup nest of vegetation is lined with fine materials; darkly marked, blue-green eggs are ⅞ x ⅝ in; female incubates 3–5 eggs for 11–14 days.

Did You Know?

The word *zonotrichia* is Greek for "band" and "hair," a reference to the White-crowned Sparrow's head pattern.

Look For

During the breeding season, these sparrows are abundant in the subalpine willow thickets and alpine krummholz of Boulder County.

Dark-eyed Junco
Junco hyemalis

Dark-eyed Juncos usually congregate in backyards with bird feeders and sheltering conifers. They spend most of their time on the ground, snatching up seeds underneath feeders. • In winter,

"Oregon Junco"

Juncos are the most commonly seen birds at Colorado bird feeders. According to Project FeederWatch statistics, Dark-eyed Juncos are consistently reported at over 90 percent of feeders! • The junco is often called the "Snow Bird," and the species name, *hyemalis*, means "winter" in Greek.

Other ID: *Female:* gray-brown where male is slate gray.
Size: L 6–7 in; W 9 in.
Voice: song is a long, dry trill; call is a smacking *chip* note, often given in series.
Status: common winter resident on the eastern plains; fairly common year-round at higher elevations.
Habitat: shrubby woodland borders and backyard feeders.

Similar Birds

Spotted Towhee
(p. 194)

Look For

This bird will flash its distinctive white outer tail feathers as it rushes for cover after being flushed.

pale pink bill

dark slate
gray overall

white outer tail
feathers

♂

white belly and
undertail coverts

"Slate-colored Junco"

Nesting: on the ground, usually concealed; female builds a cup nest of twigs, grass, bark shreds and moss; brown-marked, whitish to bluish eggs are ¾ x ½ in; female incubates 3–5 eggs for 12–13 days.

Did You Know?

There are five closely related Dark-eyed Junco subspecies in North America that share similar habits but differ in coloration and range. Four of the five subspecies are found within Colorado—all four subspecies are present in winter, but only the Gray-headed subspecies breeds in Colorado, in the foothills and mountains.

Black-headed Grosbeak
Pheucticus melanocephalus

Black-headed Grosbeaks are marvelous singers, advertising breeding territories with extended bouts of complex, accented caroling. Males sing from slightly sheltered perches near the top of a tree, while females forage and conduct nesting chores within the cover of interior foliage, betraying their presence with frequent callnotes. • Black-headed Grosbeaks are most characteristic of riparian thickets, rich oak woodlands and broken conifer forests with a strong hardwood component, but they will also visit backyard feeders adjacent to dense woodlots.

Other ID: finchlike. *Female:* dark brown upperparts; buffy underparts; lightly streaked flanks; pale eyebrow and crown stripe.
Size: L 7–8½ in; W 12½ in.
Voice: song is a loud, ecstatic caroling known for its exceptionally rich quality and its many accented notes; call is a high-pitched, penetrating *eek.*
Status: fairly common summer resident in the foothills and lower mountains.
Habitat: deciduous riparian, oak or mixed oak-coniferous woodlands, farmyards, parks and suburban tree groves.

Similar Birds

Baltimore Oriole

Purple Finch

Spotted Towhee (p. 194)

large, bicolored, conical bill

black head, back and wings

♀

white wing bars

burnt orange underparts

♂

Nesting: in a tall shrub or deciduous tree, often near water; female builds a loose cup of twigs lined with fine grass; eggs are $1\frac{1}{8}$ x $\frac{11}{16}$ in; pair incubates 3–5 eggs for 12–14 days.

Did You Know?

The scientific name *Pheucticus* is derived from the Greek *phycticos*, meaning "painted with cosmetics"; *melanocephalus* is Greek for "black-headed."

Look For

The female Black-headed Grosbeak's lemon yellow wing linings and buffy breast, eye stripe and crown stripe distinguish it from the female Rose-breasted Grosbeak.

Blue Grosbeak
Passerina caerulea

Male Blue Grosbeaks owe their spectacular spring plumage not to a fresh molt but, oddly enough, to feather wear. While Blue Grosbeaks are wintering in Mexico or Central America, their brown feather tips slowly wear away, leaving the crystal blue plumage that is seen as they arrive on their breeding grounds. The lovely blue color of the plumage is not produced by pigmentation, but by the feather structure, which reflects only short wavelengths in the light spectrum. *Caerulea* is from the Latin for "blue," a description that just doesn't grasp this bird's true beauty.

Other ID: *Male:* black around base of bill. *Female:* whitish throat; rump and shoulders are faintly washed with blue. *1st-spring male:* similar to female but has a blue head.

Size: L 6–7½ in; W 11 in.

Voice: sweet, melodious, warbling song with phrases that rise and fall; call is a loud *chink*.

Status: fairly common summer resident, especially in the southeast.

Habitat: thick brush, riparian thickets, shrubby areas and dense weedy fields near water.

Similar Birds

Indigo Bunting

Look For

A pair of rusty wing bars, visible even on first-winter birds, distinguishes the Blue Grosbeak from the similar-looking and much more common Indigo Bunting.

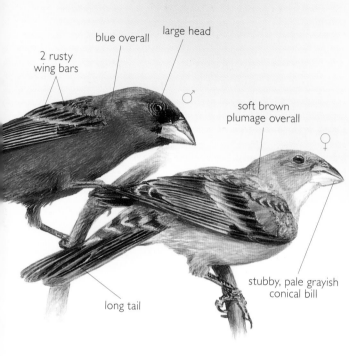

2 rusty wing bars

blue overall

large head

♂

soft brown plumage overall

♀

stubby, pale grayish conical bill

long tail

Nesting: in a shrub or low tree; cup nest is woven with twigs, roots and grass and is lined with finer materials, including paper and occasionally shed reptile skins; pale blue eggs are ⅞ x ⅝ in; female incubates 2–5 eggs for 11–12 days.

Did You Know?

The Blue Grosbeak's large bill is well designed for handling the large insects, such as grasshoppers, crickets and beetles, that are its preferred prey. Watch for this beautiful bird perched on an electrical wire, searching for its next meal.

Lazuli Bunting
Passerina amoena

Lazuli Buntings nest in open shrubby country and are most common in our foothills and mesas. Males set up territorial districts in which neighboring males copy and learn songs from one another, producing "song territories." Each male within a song territory sings with slight differences in the syllables, producing his own acoustic fingerprint. • Before migrating south, Lazuli Buntings undergo an incomplete molt of certain body feathers. They then fly to the American Southwest and to northwestern Mexico to complete their molt during the short-lived "Mexican monsoon" of late summer.

Other ID: stout, conical bill. *Female:* soft brown overall; hints of blue on rump.
Size: L 5½; W 8¾ in.
Voice: song is a variable series of wiry, piercing notes, *swip-swip-swip zu zu ee, see see sip see see*; call is a strong, dry *chip*.
Status: fairly common summer resident in the foothills and mesas.
Habitat: open brushy areas, forest edges, riparian thickets, young burns, hedges and willow and alder shrublands.

Similar Birds

Eastern Bluebird

Indigo Bunting

Blue Grosbeak
(p. 208)

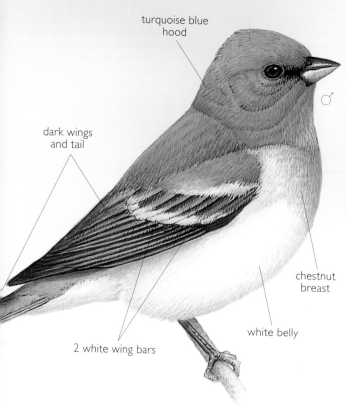

turquoise blue hood

♂

dark wings and tail

chestnut breast

white belly

2 white wing bars

Nesting: in an upright crotch low in a shrubby tangle; female weaves a small cup of grass and lines it with finer grass and hair; bluish white eggs are ¾ x ⁹⁄₁₆ in; female incubates 3–5 eggs for 12 days.

Did You Know?

This bird is named after the colorful gemstone lapis lazuli, generally pronounced as "LAZZ-you-lie."

Look For

Hybrids of Lazuli and Indigo buntings are occasionally found in northeastern Colorado.

Red-winged Blackbird
Agelaius phoeniceus

The male Red-winged Blackbird's bright red shoulders and short, raspy song are key attributes in defending his territory from rivals. In field experiments, males whose red shoulders were painted black soon lost their territories. • Nearly every cattail marsh worthy of description in Colorado plays host to Red-winged Blackbirds during at least part of the year. • Some scientists believe that this blackbird is the most abundant bird species in North America.

Other ID: *Male:* black overall. *Female:* mottled brown upperparts; pale eyebrow.
Size: *L* 7½–9 in; *W* 13 in.
Voice: song is a loud, raspy *konk-a-ree* or *ogle-reeeee*; calls include a harsh *check* and high *tseert*; female gives a loud *che-che-che chee chee chee.*
Status: abundant year-round resident at lower elevations; fairly common elsewhere, but often moves to low elevations in winter.
Habitat: cattail marshes, wet meadows and ditches, croplands and shoreline shrubs.

Similar Birds

Brewer's Blackbird

Rusty Blackbird

Brown-headed Cowbird (p. 218)

faint, red
shoulder patch

red shoulder
patch edged
in yellow

pale pinkish
throat

heavily streaked
underparts

♀

♂

Nesting: colonial; in cattails or shoreline bushes; female builds an open cup nest of dried cattail leaves and lines it with fine grass; darkly marked, pale bluish green eggs are 1 x ¾ in; female incubates 3–4 eggs for 10–12 days.

Did You Know?

Agelaius is a Greek word meaning "flocking," which describes this bird's behavior in winter, when impressive flocks can be seen.

Look For

As he sings his *konk-a-ree* song, the male Red-winged Blackbird spreads his shoulders to display his bright red wing patch to rivals and potential mates.

Western Meadowlark

Sturnella neglecta

In the early 19th century, members of the Lewis and Clark Expedition overlooked the Western Meadowlark, mistaking it for the very similar-looking Eastern Meadowlark, hence the scientific name *neglecta*. Distinguishing these two species is extremely challenging. Western Meadowlarks do prefer drier, more barren grasslands compared with the wetter habitat of the Eastern, but the different songs are probably the most accurate way to distinguish these species.

Other ID: *Breeding:* mottled brown upperparts; pale eyebrow and median crown stripe; yellow lores; short, wide tail with white outer tail feathers. *Nonbreeding:* paler plumage.
Size: L 9–9½ in; W 14½ in.
Voice: song is a rich, melodic series of bubbly, flutelike notes; calls include a low, loud *chuck* or *chup,* a rattling flight call or a few clear, whistled notes.
Status: abundant year-round resident on the eastern plains and western valleys; fairly common in the mountains.
Habitat: grassy meadows, native prairie and pastures; also in some croplands, weedy fields and grassy roadsides.

Similar Birds

Eastern Meadowlark

Dickcissel

brown crown stripes and eye line

long, sharp bill

dark streaking on white sides and flanks

broad, black breast band

yellow underparts

breeding

Nesting: in a depression or scrape on the ground in dense grass; domed grass nest with side entrance is woven into surrounding vegetation; brown- and purple-spotted, white eggs are 1⅛ x ⅞ in; female incubates 3–7 eggs for 13–15 days.

Did You Know?

Eastern Meadowlarks and Western Meadowlarks may occasionally interbreed where their ranges overlap, but their offspring are infertile.

Look For

Watch for the Western Meadowlark's courtship dance. Potential partners face each other, raise their bills high in the air and perform a grassland ballet.

Yellow-headed Blackbird
Xanthocephalus xanthocephalus

You might be taken aback by the pitiful grinding sound produced when the male Yellow-headed Blackbird perches on a cattail stalk and arches his dazzling golden head backward to "sing." • Yellow-headed Blackbirds are strategic in sharing their soggy habitat with the smaller Red-winged Blackbirds; Yellow-heads tend to command the center of the wetland, pushing competitors to the periphery where predation is highest.

Other ID: yellow breast. *Male:* black body; black lores; black bill; long tail. *Female:* dusky brown overall.
Size: L 9–11 in; W 14–15 in.
Voice: low, hoarse grating song; call is a deep *kack* or *kruck*.
Status: abundant summer resident in river valleys.
Habitat: deep marshes, sloughs, lakeshores and river impoundments where cattails dominate; will also forage on upland fields, pastures and grasslands.

Similar Birds

Rusty Blackbird

Brewer's Blackbird

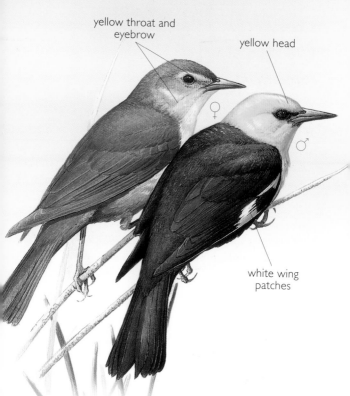

yellow throat and eyebrow

yellow head

♀

♂

white wing patches

Nesting: loosely colonial; female builds a deep basket of aquatic plants lined with dry grass, woven into surrounding vegetation over water; gray- or brown-marked, pale green to gray eggs are 1 x ¾ in; female incubates 4 eggs for 11–13 days.

Did You Know?

The Yellow-headed Blackbird requires a marsh with a 50:50 ratio of emergent vegetation and water in which to breed.

Look For

These blackbirds often nest in small colonies of about 30 pairs. The yellow heads of the males turn fields the color of mustard.

Brown-headed Cowbird

Molothrus ater

These nomads historically followed bison herds across the Great Plains (they now follow cattle), so they never stayed in one area long enough to build and tend a nest. Instead, cowbirds lay their eggs in other birds' nests, relying on the unsuspecting adoptive parents to incubate the eggs and feed the aggressive young. Orioles, warblers, vireos and tanagers are among the most affected species. Increased livestock farming and fragmentation of forests has encouraged the expansion of the cowbird's range. It is known to parasitize more than 140 bird species.

Other ID: dark eyes; thick, conical bill; short, squared tail.
Size: L 6–8 in; W 12 in.
Voice: song is a high, liquidy gurgle: *glug-ahl-whee* or *bub-bloozeee*; call is a squeaky, high-pitched *seep*, *psee* or *wee-tse-tse* or fast, chipping *ch-ch-ch-ch-ch-ch*.
Status: fairly common summer resident, except at the highest elevations.
Habitat: agricultural and residential areas, usually fields, woodland edges, utility cutlines, roadsides and fencelines.

Similar Birds

Rusty Blackbird

Brewer's Blackbird

Red-winged Blackbird
(p. 212)

pale throat

dark brown head

light brown
underparts with
faint streaking

♀

iridescent, green-
blue plumage looks
glossy black

♂

Nesting: does not build a nest; female lays up to 40 eggs a year in the nests of other birds, usually 1 egg per nest; brown-speckled, whitish eggs are ⅞ x ⅝ in; eggs hatch after 10–13 days.

Did You Know?

When courting a female, the male cowbird points his bill upward to the sky, fans his tail and wings and utters a loud *squeek*.

Look For

When cowbirds feed in flocks, they hold their back ends up high, with their tails sticking straight up in the air.

Bullock's Oriole

Icterus bullockii

Although Bullock's Orioles are common and widespread in much of Colorado, most residents are unaware of them. The male's colorful plumage blends remarkably well with the dappled light of the bird's upper-canopy summer home. Finding the drab olive, gray and white female is even more difficult. • The Bullock's Oriole and the Baltimore Oriole of eastern North America differ in vocalizations, appearance and behavior. However, they were once lumped together as a single species, the "Northern Oriole," because they hybridize in the Great Plains. Baltimore Orioles are found in the extreme northeastern corner of Colorado.

Other ID: *Male:* bright orange underparts. *Female:* gray underparts; olive gray upperparts and tail; thin, white wing bars.
Size: *L* 9 in; *W* 12 in.
Voice: song is an accented, piping series of 6–8 whistled, rich and guttural notes: *peas-n-tea, Drink-'em, Drink-'em!*
Status: common summer resident on the eastern plains and western valleys.
Habitat: riparian woodlands with large cottonwoods, willows and sycamores; oak canyons with large, well-spaced trees; suburban parks and gardens, isolated tree groves and shelter-belts in farmyards.

Similar Birds

Baltimore Oriole

Black-headed
Grosbeak (p. 206)

Western Tanager
(p. 190)

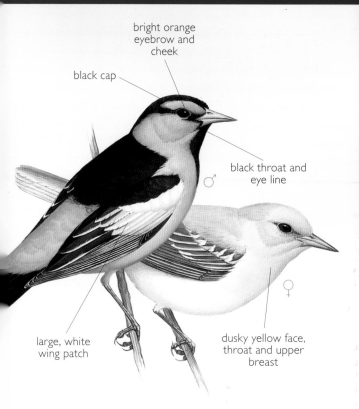

bright orange eyebrow and cheek

black cap

black throat and eye line

♂

large, white wing patch

♀

dusky yellow face, throat and upper breast

Nesting: pouch nest is suspended high in a deciduous tree and is woven with fine plant fibers, hair and string and lined with soft material; pale gray or bluish eggs with scrawling lines are 1 x ⅝ in; female incubates 4–5 eggs for 12–14 days.

Did You Know?

This bird's neatly woven nest often contains animal hair, especially horsehair.

Look For

The orioles' elaborate hanging nests become easily visible when the cottonwoods lose their leaves in fall.

Gray-crowned Rosy-Finch

Leucosticte tephrocotis

The Gray-crowned Rosy-Finch breeds on high elevation mountain slopes from Montana north to Alaska, forming small flocks on snowy alpine tundra and avalanche chutes where few other species are found. As winter approaches, this hardy bird migrates southward to the lower mountains and foothills of the northwestern United States. It frequents feeders, especially in years with heavy snowfall. • The Brown-capped Rosy-Finch and the Black Rosy-Finch also occur in Colorado.

Other ID: brown cheek, back, chin, throat and breast; dark tail and flight feathers; short, black legs. *Nonbreeding:* yellow bill.
Size: L 5½–6½ in; W 13 in.
Voice: song is long, goldfinchlike warble; calls are high, chirping notes and constant chattering.
Status: locally fairly common winter resident in the mountains.
Habitat: shrubby lower-elevation slopes, arid valleys, roadsides and townsites.

Similar Birds

Brown-capped Rosy-Finch

Black Rosy-Finch

House Finch

black forehead
and forecrown

dark, conical
bill

conspicuous gray
hindcrown

rosy shoulder,
rump and belly

breeding

Nesting: does not breed in Colorado; breeds in northwestern North America; on the ground, among rocks or in rock crevices; rarely in abandoned buildings; female builds a bulky nest of moss, grass, fur and feathers; creamy white eggs, sometimes speckled, are ⅞ x ⅝ in; female incubates 4–5 eggs for 12–14 days.

Did You Know?

Rosy-finches nest on high mountain slopes and probably breed at higher elevations than any other North American bird.

Look For

During winter, these birds are known to roost at night in caves, tunnels, abandoned buildings, mine shafts and abandoned Cliff Swallow nests.

Pine Siskin
Carduelis pinus

Pine Siskins are unpredictable, social birds that may be abundant for a time, then suddenly disappear. Because their favored habitats are widely scattered, flocks are constantly on the move, searching forests for the most lucrative seed crops. These drab, sparrowlike birds are easy to overlook at first, but once you recognize their characteristic rising *zzzreeeee* calls and boisterous chatter, you will encounter them with surprising frequency. They often feed near treetops, favoring coniferous and mixed woodlands and forest edges. They also visit bird feeders.

Other ID: dull wing bars; indistinct facial pattern.
Size: *L* 4½–5½ in; *W* 9 in.
Voice: song is a variable, bubbly mix of squeaky, raspy, metallic notes, sometimes resembling a jerky laugh; call is a buzzy, rising zzzreeeee.
Status: irregular, common year-round resident in the foothills and mountains; irregular visitor in winter thoughout Colorado.
Habitat: coniferous and mixed forests, forest edges, meadows, roadsides, agricultural fields and backyards with feeders.

Similar Birds

Common Redpoll

House Finch

dark, heavily
streaked upperparts

heavily streaked
underparts

yellow highlights at base of
tail feathers and on wings
(easily seen in flight)

slightly forked
tail

Nesting: usually loosely colonial; typically on
an outer branch of a conifer; female builds
a loose cup nest of twigs and grass, lined with
finer material; darkly spotted, pale blue eggs
are ⅝ x ½ in; female incubates 3–5 eggs for
about 13 days.

Did You Know?

Pine Siskins are attracted
to road salts, mineral licks
and ashes, all of which add
minerals to their diet.

Look For

The best way to meet these
birds is to set up a finch
feeder filled with black niger
seed in your backyard and
wait for them to appear.

American Goldfinch
Carduelis tristis

Like vibrant rays of sunshine, American Goldfinches cheerily flutter over weedy fields, gardens and along roadsides. It is hard to miss their jubilant *po-ta-to-chip* calls and their distinctive, undulating flight style.
• Because these acrobatic birds regularly feed while hanging upside down, finch feeders are designed with the seed-openings below the perches. These feeders discourage the more aggressive House Sparrows, which feed upright, from stealing the seeds. Use niger (thistle) seeds or black-oil sunflower seeds to attract American Goldfinches to your bird feeder.

Other ID: *Female:* yellow throat and breast; yellow-green belly. *Nonbreeding male:* olive brown back; yellow-tinged head; gray underparts.
Size: L 4½–5 in; W 9 in.
Voice: song is a long, varied series of trills, twitters, warbles and hissing notes; calls include *po-ta-to-chip* or *per-chic-or-ee* (often delivered in flight) and a whistled *dear-me, see-me.*
Status: fairly common winter resident and uncommon summer resident in the eastern plains and western valleys.
Habitat: weedy fields, woodland edges, meadows, riparian areas, parks and gardens.

Similar Birds

Evening Grosbeak

Wilson's Warbler
(p. 186)

yellow-green
upperparts

black cap
extends onto
forehead

black wings
with white
wing bars

♀

orange bill

♂

white rump
and undertail
coverts

orange legs

breeding

Nesting: in the fork of a deciduous tree; compact cup nest of plant fibers, grass and spider silk; pale bluish eggs are ⅝ x ½ in; female incubates 4–6 eggs for 12–14 days.

Did You Know?

These birds nest in late summer to ensure that there is a dependable source of seeds from thistles and dandelions to feed their young.

Look For

American Goldfinches delight in perching on late-summer thistle heads or poking through dandelion patches in search of seeds.

House Sparrow
Passer domesticus

A black mask and "bib" adorn the male of this adaptive, aggressive species. The House Sparrow's tendency to usurp territory has led to a decline in native bird populations. This sparrow will even help itself to the convenience of another bird's home, such as a bluebird or Cliff Swallow nest or a Purple Martin house. • This abundant and conspicuous bird was introduced to North America in the 1850s as part of a plan to control the insects that were damaging grain and cereal crops. As it turns out, these birds are largely vegetarian!

Other ID: *Breeding male:* gray crown; black bill; dark, mottled upperparts; gray underparts; white wing bar. *Female:* indistinct facial patterns; plain gray-brown overall; streaked upperparts; grayish, unstreaked underparts.
Size: L 5½–6½ in; W 9½ in.
Voice: song is a plain, familiar *cheep-cheep-cheep-cheep;* call is a short *chill-up.*
Status: abundant year-round resident, except at the highest elevations.
Habitat: townsites, urban and suburban areas, farmyards and agricultural areas, railroad yards and other developed areas.

Similar Birds

Harris's Sparrow

Look For

In spring, House Sparrows feast on the buds of fruit trees and will sometimes eat lettuce from your backyard garden.

buffy eyebrow

chestnut nape

black lore
and "bib"

light gray
cheek

♀

♂

breeding

Nesting: often communal; in a birdhouse, ornamental shrub or natural cavity; pair builds a large
dome nest of grass, twigs and plant fibers; gray-
speckled, white to greenish eggs are ⅞ x ⅝ in;
pair incubates 4–6 eggs for 10–13 days.

Did You Know?

The House Sparrow successfully established itself in North
Amercia over a relatively short period of time, owing in part
to its high reproductive output. A pair may raise up to four
clutches per year, with up to eight young per clutch.

Glossary

brood: *n.* a family of young from one hatching; *v.* to sit on eggs so as to hatch them.

buteo: a high-soaring hawk (genus *Buteo*); characterized by broad wings and short, wide tails; feeds mostly on small mammals and other land animals.

cere: a fleshy area at the base of a bird's bill that contains the nostrils.

clutch: the number of eggs laid by the female at one time.

corvid: a member of the crow family (Corvidae); includes crows, jays, ravens and magpies.

covey: a group of birds, usually grouse or quail.

crop: an enlargement of the esophagus; serves as a storage structure and (in pigeons) has glands that produce secretions.

cryptic: a coloration pattern that helps to conceal the bird.

dabbling: a foraging technique used by ducks, in which the head and neck are submerged but the body and tail remain on the water's surface; dabbling ducks can usually walk easily on land, can take off without running and have brightly colored speculums.

endangered: facing imminent extirpation or extinction.

fledgling: a young bird that has left the nest but is dependent upon its parents.

flushing: a behavior in which frightened birds explode into flight in response to a disturbance.

flycatching: a feeding behavior in which the bird leaves a perch, snatches an insect in midair and returns to the same perch.

hawking: attempting to catch insects through aerial pursuit.

leading edge: the front edge of the wing as viewed from below.

mantle: feathers of the back and upperside of folded wings.

morph: one of several alternate plumages displayed by members of a species.

nocturnal: active during the night.

primaries: the outermost flight feathers.

raptor: a carnivorous (meat-eating) bird; includes eagles, hawks, falcons and owls.

riparian: refers to habitat along riverbanks.

rufous: rusty red in color.

special concern: a species that has characteristics that make it particularly sensitive to human activities or disturbance, requires a very specific or unique habitat or whose status is such that it requires careful monitoring.

speculum: a brightly colored patch on the wings of many dabbling ducks.

stoop: a steep dive through the air, usually performed by birds of prey while foraging or during courtship displays.

threatened: likely to become endangered in the near future in all or part of its range.

Checklist

The following checklist contains 345 species of birds that have been officially recorded as regular in Colorado. Species are grouped by family and listed in taxonomic order in accordance with the American Ornithologists' Union's *Check-list of North American Birds* (7th ed.) and its supplements. In addition, the following risk categories are noted: endangered (en), threatened (th) and special concern (sc). In some cases only certain subspecies (ssp) are at risk.

We wish to thank the Colorado Field Ornithologists for their kind assistance in providing the information for this checklist.

Waterfowl
❏ Greater White-fronted Goose
❏ Snow Goose
❏ Ross's Goose
❏ Cackling Goose
❏ Canada Goose
❏ Wood Duck
❏ Gadwall
❏ American Wigeon
❏ Mallard
❏ Blue-winged Teal
❏ Cinnamon Teal
❏ Northern Shoveler
❏ Northern Pintail
❏ Green-winged Teal
❏ Canvasback
❏ Redhead
❏ Ring-necked Duck
❏ Greater Scaup
❏ Lesser Scaup
❏ Surf Scoter
❏ White-winged Scoter
❏ Black Scoter
❏ Long-tailed Duck
❏ Bufflehead
❏ Common Goldeneye
❏ Barrow's Goldeneye
❏ Hooded Merganser
❏ Common Merganser
❏ Red-breasted Merganser
❏ Ruddy Duck

Grouse & Allies
❏ Chukar
❏ Ring-necked Pheasant
❏ Greater Sage-Grouse (sc)
❏ Gunnison Sage-Grouse (sc)
❏ White-tailed Ptarmigan
❏ Dusky Grouse
❏ Sharp-tailed Grouse (*columbianus* ssp: sc; *jamesii* ssp: en)
❏ Greater Prairie-Chicken
❏ Lesser Prairie-Chicken (th)
❏ Wild Turkey

Quails
❏ Northern Bobwhite
❏ Scaled Quail
❏ Gambel's Quail

Loons
❏ Pacific Loon
❏ Common Loon

Grebes
❏ Pied-billed Grebe
❏ Horned Grebe
❏ Red-necked Grebe
❏ Eared Grebe
❏ Western Grebe
❏ Clark's Grebe

Pelicans
❏ American White Pelican

Cormorants
❏ Double-crested Cormorant

Herons & Allies
❏ American Bittern
❏ Great Blue Heron
❏ Great Egret
❏ Snowy Egret
❏ Little Blue Heron
❏ Cattle Egret
❏ Green Heron
❏ Black-crowned Night-Heron

Ibises
❏ White-faced Ibis

Vultures
❏ Turkey Vulture

Hawks & Eagles
❏ Osprey
❏ Mississippi Kite
❏ Bald Eagle (th)
❏ Northern Harrier
❏ Sharp-shinned Hawk
❏ Cooper's Hawk
❏ Northern Goshawk
❏ Broad-winged Hawk
❏ Swainson's Hawk
❏ Red-tailed Hawk
❏ Ferruginous Hawk (sc)
❏ Rough-legged Hawk
❏ Golden Eagle

Falcons
❏ American Kestrel
❏ Merlin
❏ Peregrine Falcon (sc)
❏ Prairie Falcon

Rails & Coots
❏ Black Rail
❏ Virginia Rail
❏ Sora
❏ American Coot

Cranes
❏ Sandhill Crane (greater ssp: sc)

Plovers
❏ Black-bellied Plover
❏ American Golden-Plover
❏ Snowy Plover (sc)
❏ Semipalmated Plover
❏ Piping Plover (th)
❏ Killdeer
❏ Mountain Plover (sc)

Stilts & Avocets
❏ Black-necked Stilt
❏ American Avocet

Sandpipers & Allies
❏ Spotted Sandpiper
❏ Solitary Sandpiper
❏ Greater Yellowlegs
❏ Willet
❏ Lesser Yellowlegs
❏ Upland Sandpiper
❏ Whimbrel
❏ Long-billed Curlew (sc)
❏ Marbled Godwit
❏ Ruddy Turnstone
❏ Sanderling
❏ Semipalmated Sandpiper
❏ Western Sandpiper
❏ Least Sandpiper
❏ White-rumped Sandpiper
❏ Baird's Sandpiper
❏ Pectoral Sandpiper
❏ Dunlin

- ❑ Stilt Sandpiper
- ❑ Short-billed Dowitcher
- ❑ Long-billed Dowitcher
- ❑ Wilson's Snipe
- ❑ Wilson's Phalarope
- ❑ Red-necked Phalarope

Gulls & Allies
- ❑ Franklin's Gull
- ❑ Bonaparte's Gull
- ❑ Ring-billed Gull
- ❑ California Gull
- ❑ Herring Gull
- ❑ Thayer's Gull
- ❑ Lesser Black-backed Gull
- ❑ Glaucous Gull
- ❑ Sabine's Gull
- ❑ Least Tern (en)
- ❑ Caspian Tern
- ❑ Black Tern
- ❑ Common Tern
- ❑ Forster's Tern

Pigeons & Doves
- ❑ Rock Pigeon
- ❑ Band-tailed Pigeon
- ❑ Eurasian Collared-Dove
- ❑ White-winged Dove
- ❑ Mourning Dove

Cuckoos & Roadrunners
- ❑ Yellow-billed Cuckoo (sc)
- ❑ Greater Roadrunner

Barn Owls
- ❑ Barn Owl

Typical Owls
- ❑ Flammulated Owl
- ❑ Western Screech-Owl
- ❑ Eastern Screech-Owl
- ❑ Great Horned Owl
- ❑ Northern Pygmy-Owl
- ❑ Burrowing Owl (th)
- ❑ Spotted Owl (*lucida* ssp: th)
- ❑ Long-eared Owl
- ❑ Short-eared Owl
- ❑ Boreal Owl
- ❑ Northern Saw-whet Owl

Nightjars
- ❑ Common Nighthawk
- ❑ Common Poorwill

Swifts
- ❑ Black Swift
- ❑ Chimney Swift
- ❑ White-throated Swift

Hummingbirds
- ❑ Black-chinned Hummingbird
- ❑ Calliope Hummingbird
- ❑ Broad-tailed Hummingbird
- ❑ Rufous Hummingbird

Kingfishers
- ❑ Belted Kingfisher

Woodpeckers
- ❑ Lewis's Woodpecker
- ❑ Red-headed Woodpecker
- ❑ Red-bellied Woodpecker
- ❑ Williamson's Sapsucker
- ❑ Red-naped Sapsucker
- ❑ Ladder-backed Woodpecker
- ❑ Downy Woodpecker
- ❑ Hairy Woodpecker
- ❑ American Three-toed Woodpecker
- ❑ Northern Flicker

Flycatchers
- ❑ Olive-sided Flycatcher
- ❑ Western Wood-Pewee
- ❑ Willow Flycatcher (*extimus* ssp: en)
- ❑ Least Flycatcher
- ❑ Hammond's Flycatcher
- ❑ Gray Flycatcher
- ❑ Ducky Flycatcher
- ❑ Cordilleran Flycatcher
- ❑ Black Phoebe
- ❑ Eastern Phoebe
- ❑ Say's Phoebe
- ❑ Ash-throated Flycatcher
- ❑ Great Crested Flycatcher
- ❑ Cassin's Kingbird
- ❑ Western Kingbird
- ❑ Eastern Kingbird

Shrikes
❏ Loggerhead Shrike
❏ Northern Shrike

Vireos
❏ White-eyed Vireo
❏ Bell's Vireo
❏ Gray Vireo
❏ Yellow-throated Vireo
❏ Plumbeous Vireo
❏ Cassin's Vireo
❏ Warbling Vireo
❏ Red-eyed Vireo

Jays & Crows
❏ Gray Jay
❏ Steller's Jay
❏ Blue Jay
❏ Western Scrub-Jay
❏ Pinyon Jay
❏ Clark's Nutcracker
❏ Black-billed Magpie
❏ American Crow
❏ Chihuahuan Raven
❏ Common Raven

Larks
❏ Horned Lark

Swallows
❏ Purple Martin
❏ Tree Swallow
❏ Violet-green Swallow
❏ Northern Rough-winged
  Swallow
❏ Bank Swallow
❏ Cliff Swallow
❏ Barn Swallow

Chickadees & Titmice
❏ Black-capped Chickadee
❏ Mountain Chickadee
❏ Juniper Titmouse
❏ Bushtit

Nuthatches
❏ Red-breasted Nuthatch
❏ White-breasted Nuthatch
❏ Pygmy Nuthatch

Creepers
❏ Brown Creeper

Wrens
❏ Rock Wren
❏ Canyon Wren
❏ Carolina Wren
❏ Bewick's Wren
❏ House Wren
❏ Winter Wren
❏ Marsh Wren

Dippers
❏ American Dipper

Kinglets
❏ Golden-crowned Kinglet
❏ Ruby-crowned Kinglet

Gnatcatchers
❏ Blue-gray Gnatcatcher

Bluebirds & Thrushes
❏ Eastern Bluebird
❏ Western Bluebird
❏ Mountain Bluebird
❏ Townsend's Solitaire
❏ Veery
❏ Swainson's Thrush
❏ Hermit Thrush
❏ American Robin

Mimic Thrushes
❏ Gray Catbird
❏ Northern Mockingbird
❏ Sage Thrasher
❏ Brown Thrasher
❏ Curve-billed Thrasher

Starlings
❏ European Starling

Pipits
❏ American Pipit

Waxwings
❏ Bohemian Waxwing
❏ Cedar Waxwing

Wood-warblers

❏ Blue-winged Warbler
❏ Golden-winged Warbler
❏ Tennessee Warbler
❏ Orange-crowned Warbler
❏ Nashville Warbler
❏ Virginia's Warbler
❏ Northern Parula
❏ Yellow Warbler
❏ Chestnut-sided Warbler
❏ Magnolia Warbler
❏ Black-throated Blue Warbler
❏ Yellow-rumped Warbler
❏ Black-throated Gray Warbler
❏ Black-throated Green Warbler
❏ Townsend's Warbler
❏ Grace's Warbler
❏ Palm Warbler
❏ Blackpoll Warbler
❏ Black-and-white Warbler
❏ American Redstart
❏ Prothonotary Warbler
❏ Worm-eating Warbler
❏ Ovenbird
❏ Northern Waterthrush
❏ MacGillivray's Warbler
❏ Common Yellowthroat
❏ Hooded Warbler
❏ Wilson's Warbler
❏ Yellow-breasted Chat

Tanagers

❏ Summer Tanager
❏ Western Tanager

Sparrows & Allies

❏ Green-tailed Towhee
❏ Spotted Towhee
❏ Canyon Towhee
❏ Cassin's Sparrow
❏ Rufous-crowned Sparrow
❏ American Tree Sparrow
❏ Chipping Sparrow
❏ Clay-colored Sparrow
❏ Brewer's Sparrow
❏ Field Sparrow
❏ Vesper Sparrow
❏ Lark Sparrow
❏ Black-throated Sparrow
❏ Sage Sparrow
❏ Lark Bunting
❏ Savannah Sparrow
❏ Grasshopper Sparrow
❏ Fox Sparrow
❏ Song Sparrow
❏ Lincoln's Sparrow
❏ Swamp Sparrow
❏ White-throated Sparrow
❏ Harris's Sparrow
❏ White-crowned Sparrow
❏ Dark-eyed Junco
❏ McCown's Longspur
❏ Lapland Longspur
❏ Chestnut-collared Longspur
❏ Snow Bunting

Grosbeaks & Buntings

❏ Northern Cardinal
❏ Rose-breasted Grosbeak
❏ Black-headed Grosbeak
❏ Blue Grosbeak
❏ Lazuli Bunting
❏ Indigo Bunting
❏ Dickcissel

Blackbirds & Allies

❏ Bobolink
❏ Red-winged Blackbird
❏ Western Meadowlark
❏ Yellow-headed Blackbird
❏ Rusty Blackbird
❏ Brewer's Blackbird
❏ Common Grackle
❏ Great-tailed Grackle
❏ Brown-headed Cowbird
❏ Orchard Oriole
❏ Bullock's Oriole
❏ Baltimore Oriole
❏ Scott's Oriole

Finches

❏ Gray-crowned Rosy-Finch

- ❏ Black Rosy-Finch
- ❏ Brown-capped Rosy-Finch
- ❏ Pine Grosbeak
- ❏ Cassin's Finch
- ❏ House Finch
- ❏ Red Crossbill
- ❏ White-winged Crossbill

- ❏ Common Redpoll
- ❏ Pine Siskin
- ❏ Lesser Goldfinch
- ❏ American Goldfinch
- ❏ Evening Grosbeak

Old World Sparrows
- ❏ House Sparrow

Select References

American Ornithologists' Union. 1998. *Check-list of North American Birds.* 7th ed. (and its supplements). American Ornithologists' Union, Washington, D.C.

Andrews, R. & R. Righter. 1992. *Colorado Birds: A Reference to Their Distribution and Habitat.* Denver Museum of Natural History, Denver, Colorado.

National Geographic Society. 2006. *Field Guide to the Birds of North America.* 5th ed. National Geographic Society, Washington, D.C.

Sibley, D.A. 2000. *National Audubon Society: The Sibley Guide to Birds.* Alfred A. Knopf, New York.

Double-crested Cormorant

Index